Extending Bootstrap

Understand Bootstrap and unlock its secrets to build a truly customized project!

Christoffer Niska

[PACKT] PUBLISHING

open source*
community experience distilled

BIRMINGHAM - MUMBAI

Extending Bootstrap

Copyright © 2014 Packt Publishing

All rights reserved. No part of this book may be reproduced, stored in a retrieval system, or transmitted in any form or by any means, without the prior written permission of the publisher, except in the case of brief quotations embedded in critical articles or reviews.

Every effort has been made in the preparation of this book to ensure the accuracy of the information presented. However, the information contained in this book is sold without warranty, either express or implied. Neither the author, nor Packt Publishing, and its dealers and distributors will be held liable for any damages caused or alleged to be caused directly or indirectly by this book.

Packt Publishing has endeavored to provide trademark information about all of the companies and products mentioned in this book by the appropriate use of capitals. However, Packt Publishing cannot guarantee the accuracy of this information.

First published: March 2014

Production Reference: 1140314

Published by Packt Publishing Ltd.
Livery Place
35 Livery Street
Birmingham B3 2PB, UK.

ISBN 978-1-78216-841-6

www.packtpub.com

Cover Image by Suresh Mogre (suresh.mogre.99@gmail.com)

Credits

Author
Christoffer Niska

Reviewers
Maxwell Dayvson da Silva
Simo Jokela
Julien Renaux

Acquisition Editors
Akram Hussain
Owen Roberts

Content Development Editor
Priyanka S.

Technical Editors
Shweta Pant
Humera Shaikh
Ritika Singh

Copy Editors
Insiya Morbiwala
Kirti Pai
Shambhavi Pai

Project Coordinator
Aboli Ambardekar

Proofreader
Ameesha Green

Indexer
Monica Ajmera Mehta

Production Coordinator
Nitesh Thakur

Cover Work
Kyle Albuquerque

About the Author

Christoffer Niska is a web developer from Helsinki, Finland. He maintains many open source projects that are mainly extensions of the Yii PHP framework. Christoffer's most notable open source effort is Yiistrap, which is an extension for Yii that allows developers to use Twitter Bootstrap along with Yii in a very convenient way.

Christoffer is the CTO at Nord Software Ltd., a company based in Helsinki that delivers cutting-edge web solutions to various clients of all sizes. At work, he helps clients to transform their vision into reality. During his hours off from work, he maintains his open source projects, experiments with web technologies, and makes arcade games using HTML5 and JavaScript.

Christoffer's Twitter handle is `@Crisu83` and his online portfolio can be found at `http://crisu83.me`. *Extending Bootstrap* is his first official attempt at writing and very likely, not the last.

> I would like to thank my lovely wife, Pauliina, and my two amazing sons, Andreas and Samuel, for allowing me the time to work on this book. I would also like to thank and express my heartfelt gratitude to everyone at Packt Publishing for giving me the opportunity to write this book.
>
> I would also like to thank my mentor, the former CTO of Nord Software Ltd., Simon Björklund, for inspiring me to become the developer that I am today. Last but not least, I would like to express my gratitude to all my current and former colleagues at Nord Software Ltd. for everything that they have taught me over the years.

About the Reviewers

Maxwell Dayvson da Silva, a native Brazilian, works as a software engineer for The New York Times. He collectively has more than 10 years of experience after working with two of Brazil's leading digital media companies. Maxwell's work at Terra, a global digital media company, helped reach an audience of over 100 million people for monthly with entertainment, sports, and news content. Later, Maxwell was a part of `Globo.com`, the largest media conglomerate in Latin America. His contribution in the digital media field is only a portion of how Maxwell spends his time. Combining his passion for art and science, Maxwell creates games and interactive art installations. Inspired by his son, Arthur, Maxwell continually searches for new ways to spread knowledge about science in a fun way to children both in NYC and Brazil. To get to know more about him visit `https://github.com/dayvson`.

Simo Jokela is a web development professional with a solid skill set. He has strong knowledge about overall web application development but his main focus is still on frontend development. He has worked with Twitter Bootstrap from the start and will continue to do so. Simo is a lead developer at Nord Software Ltd. and is a colleague of Christoffer Niska, the author of this book.

> I would like to thank Christoffer for giving me the honor of reviewing his book, and Suvi for supporting me.

Julien Renaux is a software engineer who specializes in frontend development. Currently working in France, Julien worked in four continents for companies such as eBay Inc, where he used Bootstrap since its first release in 2011. Web passionate and a JavaScript-aholic, Julien loves to learn new technologies and share his experience and enthusiasm on his blog `http://julienrenaux.fr`.

www.PacktPub.com

Support files, eBooks, discount offers and more

You might want to visit www.PacktPub.com for support files and downloads related to your book.

Did you know that Packt offers eBook versions of every book published, with PDF and ePub files available? You can upgrade to the eBook version at www.PacktPub.com and as a print book customer, you are entitled to a discount on the eBook copy. Get in touch with us at service@packtpub.com for more details.

At www.PacktPub.com, you can also read a collection of free technical articles, sign up for a range of free newsletters and receive exclusive discounts and offers on Packt books and eBooks.

PACKTLiB

http://PacktLib.PacktPub.com

Do you need instant solutions to your IT questions? PacktLib is Packt's online digital book library. Here, you can access, read and search across Packt's entire library of books.

Why Subscribe?
- Fully searchable across every book published by Packt
- Copy and paste, print and bookmark content
- On demand and accessible via web browser

Free Access for Packt account holders

If you have an account with Packt at www.PacktPub.com, you can use this to access PacktLib today and view nine entirely free books. Simply use your login credentials for immediate access.

Table of Contents

Preface — 1

Chapter 1: Getting Started with Bootstrap — 5
- Why use Bootstrap? — 5
- Bootstrap pros and cons — 6
- Creating your first Bootstrap project — 7
- Summary — 9

Chapter 2: Applying a Custom Theme — 11
- When to use a theme — 11
- Finding a suitable theme — 13
- Applying the theme — 14
- Customizing your theme — 17
- Best practices — 21
- Summary — 22

Chapter 3: Creating Your Own Build — 23
- Need to customize Bootstrap — 23
- Generating a custom build — 24
- Keeping only what you need — 27
- Summary — 29

Chapter 4: LESS is More — 31
- Why use LESS? — 31
- Compiling your first LESS file — 32
- Building Bootstrap from the source — 33
- Customizing variables — 34
- Summary — 39

Chapter 5: Compiling Your Styles with Grunt — 41
- Why build LESS files with Grunt? — 41
- Using Grunt to build your project — 42
- Using Grunt for live reloading — 45
- Summary — 46

Chapter 6: Adapting Bootstrap JavaScript Plugins — 47
- Why customize plugins? — 47
- Customizing plugins — 48
- Extending Bootstrap plugins — 50
- Summary — 55

Chapter 7: Custom Grids — 57
- Why use a custom grid? — 57
- Customizing the grid — 58
- Custom breakpoints — 59
- Disabling responsiveness — 60
- Summary — 61

Chapter 8: Custom Bootstrap Plugins — 63
- Why use custom plugins? — 63
- Popular plugins — 63
  - Bootbox.js — 64
  - Bootstrap DateTime Picker — 64
  - Bootstrap Modal — 65
  - Bootstrap Lightbox — 66
  - Bootstrap Wysihtml5 — 66
  - Font Awesome — 67
  - Jasny Bootstrap — 67
  - jQuery File Upload — 68
  - Notify.js — 68
  - typeahead.js — 69
  - X-editable — 70
- Summary — 70

Chapter 9: Creating Your Own Theme — 71
- Why create a theme? — 71
- Creating your own Bootstrap theme — 72
- Publishing your theme — 73
- Summary — 74

Index — 75

Preface

Extending Bootstrap is a practical guide to extending the use of Bootstrap, a very popular open source CSS framework originally developed by Twitter. This book focuses on different techniques to customize and extend Bootstrap according to your needs. We will cover theming, CSS customization, LESS usage, compiling your styles with Grunt.js, and much more. After reading this book, you will be an expert in Bootstrap and have all the knowledge you need to use it efficiently in your projects.

What this book covers

Chapter 1, Getting Started with Bootstrap, helps you understand why you should use Twitter Bootstrap in the first place.

Chapter 2, Applying a Custom Theme, shows you how to create your first Bootstrap project and apply a Bootswatch theme to it.

Chapter 3, Creating Your Own Build, uses the customize tool from the Bootstrap site to create your own build of Bootstrap.

Chapter 4, LESS is More, provides an introduction to LESS, a preprocessed style sheet language that changes the way you work.

Chapter 5, Compiling Your Styles with Grunt, uses Grunt.js to compile your styles and improve your efficiency.

Chapter 6, Adapting Bootstrap JavaScript Plugins, shows you how to customize and extend Bootstrap JavaScript plugins to do more.

Chapter 7, Custom Grids, teaches you how to customize the grid in Bootstrap.

Chapter 8, Custom Bootstrap Plugins, introduces you to many useful plugins that you can use with Bootstrap.

Chapter 9, Creating Your Own Theme, teaches you how to create your own theme using Bootswatch.

What you need for this book

In order to follow the examples in this book, you will need to install a web server (XAMPP or similar), Node.js, a text editor (Sublime Text 2 or similar), and Google Chrome.

Who this book is for

If you are an intermediate or advanced web developer or designer who is interested in unlocking the secrets within Bootstrap and want to start using it for your projects, this is the book for you.

Conventions

In this book, you will find a number of styles of text that distinguish between different kinds of information. Here are some examples of these styles and an explanation of their meaning.

Code words in text, folder names, filenames, file extensions, pathnames, are shown as follows: "Create a new HTML document, add the following contents, and save it in your project directory as index.html."

A block of code is set as follows:

```
[default]
grunt.initConfig({
  less: {
    app: {
      files: {"less/main.less": "css/main.css"}
    }
  }
});
```

When we wish to draw your attention to a particular part of a code block, the relevant lines or items are set in bold:

```
[default]
grunt.initConfig({
  less: {
    app: {
      files: {"less/main.less": "css/main.css"}
    }
  }
});
```

Any command-line input or output is written as follows:

```
recess less/main.less --compile > css/main.css
```

New terms and **important** words are shown in bold. Words that you see on the screen, in menus or dialog boxes for example, appear in the text like this: "For more information, refer to the **Live Reloading** section in the Watch plugin documentation."

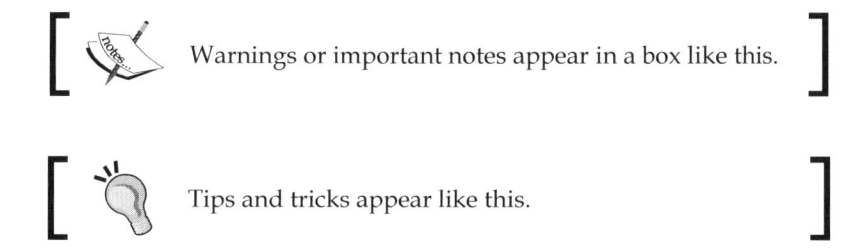

> Warnings or important notes appear in a box like this.

> Tips and tricks appear like this.

Reader feedback

Feedback from our readers is always welcome. Let us know what you think about this book—what you liked or may have disliked. Reader feedback is important for us to develop titles that you really get the most out of.

To send us general feedback, simply send an e-mail to feedback@packtpub.com, and mention the book title via the subject of your message.

If there is a topic that you have expertise in and you are interested in either writing or contributing to a book, see our author guide on www.packtpub.com/authors.

Customer support

Now that you are the proud owner of a Packt book, we have a number of things to help you to get the most from your purchase.

Downloading the example code

You can download the example code files for all Packt books you have purchased from your account at http://www.packtpub.com. If you purchased this book elsewhere, you can visit http://www.packtpub.com/support and register to have the files e-mailed directly to you.

Errata

Although we have taken every care to ensure the accuracy of our content, mistakes do happen. If you find a mistake in one of our books—maybe a mistake in the text or the code—we would be grateful if you would report this to us. By doing so, you can save other readers from frustration and help us improve subsequent versions of this book. If you find any errata, please report them by visiting http://www.packtpub.com/submit-errata, selecting your book, clicking on the **errata submission form** link, and entering the details of your errata. Once your errata are verified, your submission will be accepted and the errata will be uploaded on our website, or added to any list of existing errata, under the Errata section of that title. Any existing errata can be viewed by selecting your title from http://www.packtpub.com/support.

Piracy

Piracy of copyright material on the Internet is an ongoing problem across all media. At Packt, we take the protection of our copyright and licenses very seriously. If you come across any illegal copies of our works, in any form, on the Internet, please provide us with the location address or website name immediately so that we can pursue a remedy.

Please contact us at copyright@packtpub.com with a link to the suspected pirated material.

We appreciate your help in protecting our authors, and our ability to bring you valuable content.

Questions

You can contact us at questions@packtpub.com if you are having a problem with any aspect of the book, and we will do our best to address it.

1
Getting Started with Bootstrap

You must be eager to start your first Bootstrap project, but hold your horses. First, you will need to learn a few useful things about Bootstrap in order to know whether or not Bootstrap is a good suite for your project.

Why use Bootstrap?

Twitter Bootstrap is an excellent CSS framework that provides many carefully crafted user interface elements, layouts, and jQuery plugins. Bootstrap is open source and is also one of the most popular projects of all time on GitHub.

Bootstrap contains a top-notch, responsive mobile-first grid, which allows you to implement your design in a breeze; it comes with ready-made styles for typography, navigation, tables, forms, buttons, and more.

Bootstrap also includes some jQuery plugins, such as Modal, Dropdown, Tooltip, and Carousel, which come in handy quite often.

> *Today, you can use Bootstrap to throw together quick prototypes or guide the execution of more sophisticated designs and larger engineering efforts. In other words, Bootstrap is a very simple way to promote quick, clean and highly usable applications.*
>
> *– Mark Otto, creator of Bootstrap*

Even though Bootstrap comes with all these features, none of them actually get in the way of further customization. Bootstrap is very easy to extend, especially if you use LESS instead of traditional CSS.

> *At its core, Bootstrap is just CSS, but it's built with Less, a flexible pre-processor that offers much more power and flexibility than regular CSS. With Less, we gain a range of features like nested declarations, variables, mixins, operations, and color functions.*
>
> *– Mark Otto, creator of Bootstrap*

Next, you will learn about the advantages and disadvantages of using Bootstrap.

Bootstrap pros and cons

As with many things, using Bootstrap too has its pros and cons. Let us list some important things that you will need to know when you decide whether or not to use Bootstrap in your project.

The pros are as follows:

- **Cross-browser support**: Bootstrap works on all the latest desktop and mobile browsers. While older browsers may display Bootstrap differently with respect to styles, it is still fully functional in legacy browsers such as Internet Explorer 8.
- **Easy to customize**: Bootstrap is easy to customize, especially with the use of LESS. You can also leave out parts that you do not need, that is, you can use only its grid and leave out all the components, or you can leave out the grid and use its components.
- **Encourages using LESS**: Bootstrap is written in LESS, a dynamic style sheet language that is compiled into CSS, which gives it a lot of flexibility. You can take advantage of this if you use LESS to write your styles.
- **Supports useful jQuery plugins**: Bootstrap comes with many useful jQuery plugins that can come handy in many situations. The quality of the plugins is not the best, and they usually work best when you do not customize them at all.
- **Many custom jQuery plugins available**: There is a wide range of jQuery plugins that extend Bootstrap, for example, X-editable, Wysihtml5, and the jQuery File Upload. We will cover these plugins later in this book.
- **Mobile-first**: Bootstrap has been mobile-first since Version 3.0. This means that the grid starts out stacked and is floated using media queries when the screen width grows.

The cons are as follows:

- **jQuery plugins are hard to customize**: The jQuery plugins that come with Bootstrap are often hard to customize, and many argue that they are not written using best practices, so it can be challenging to work with the source code at times. Usually, the plugins work in the most common cases but they come up short when you try to customize them a bit.
- **Many Bootstrap sites end up looking alike**: It is unfortunate that many sites that are built with Bootstrap look exactly the same, but you can avoid this by using a custom theme or creating your own theme once you have read this book.

> **Downloading the example code**
> You can download the sample code files for all Packt books that you have purchased from your account at http://www.packtpub.com. If you purchased this book elsewhere, you can visit http://www.packtpub.com/support and register to have the files e-mailed directly to you.

Creating your first Bootstrap project

Now that you know when it is suitable to use Bootstrap, you are ready to start your first Bootstrap project. Perform the following steps to get started:

1. Create a new folder for your Bootstrap project inside your document root. You can call it `bootstrap-app`.
2. Pick up the latest version of Bootstrap from `http://getbootstrap.com` and unpack it into your project directory.
3. Create a new HTML document, add the following contents, and save it in your project directory as `index.html` in the following manner:

```
<!DOCTYPE html>
<html>
  <head>
    <title>Hello from Bootstrap</title>
    <!-- Ensure proper rendering and touch zooming on mobile devices -->
    <meta name="viewport" content="width=device-width, initial-scale=1.0">
```

```html
      <link href="css/bootstrap.min.css" rel="stylesheet">
      <!-- HTML5 Shim and Respond.js IE8 support of HTML5 elements
      and media queries -->
      <!--[if lt IE 9]>
        <script src="https://oss.maxcdn.com/libs/html5shiv/3.7.0/
        html5shiv.js"></script>
        <script src="https://oss.maxcdn.com/libs/respond.js/1.3.0/
        respond.min.js"></script>
      <![endif]-->
  </head>
  <body>
    <h1>Hello, world!</h1>
  </body>
</html>
```

> You can omit `html5shiv.js` and `respond.js` if you don't wish to support older versions of Internet Explorer.

Let us look at the following reasons why we included all those CSS and JavaScript files:

- `bootstrap.min.css`: It is the minified version of the Bootstrap CSS styles
- `html5shiv.js`: It adds HTML5 support to older browsers
- `respond.min.js`: It adds media query support to older browsers

Navigate to your project directory using your favorite web browser; you should see your project in action as shown in the following screenshot. Not too impressive, but do not worry, you will soon add more to it.

Hello, world!

> For more information on how to get started with Bootstrap, refer to the **Getting started** page on the official site at `http://getbootstrap.com/getting-started/`.

Summary

You now know why you should use Bootstrap in your projects rather than writing all the CSS files yourself, and you know what kind of features Bootstrap provides.

In this chapter, you learned about the pros and cons of Bootstrap, as well as how to decide whether or not to use Bootstrap in a project. You also learned how to create a very simple Bootstrap project.

The project you created in this chapter was not so impressive; it was just some dark text on a white background. In the next chapter, you will learn how to apply a custom theme to your newly created Bootstrap project. Onwards!

2
Applying a Custom Theme

Themes are an easy way to customize your project. There are numerous free and paid themes available for Bootstrap. In this chapter, you will learn where to find themes and how to choose a suitable one and adapt it to your project.

When to use a theme

Now that you have learned a bit about Bootstrap, it is time you learn about the difference between a professional website built with Bootstrap and an amateur one. The most common mistake that developers make is using Bootstrap as it is and not customizing it at all. This is the main reason why many websites today look alike, and that is not a good thing.

Applying a Custom Theme

It is almost like most developers forgot about designers the moment they started to use Bootstrap on their website because they thought that it looked awesome with its default styles. The following screenshot clearly illustrates how similar Bootstrap sites can look:

Of course, this is wrong. The default styles are just that, *default*. In order to give a professional feel to a website, you need to customize Bootstrap to some extent. Keep in mind that CSS frameworks are only a base for your styles, not the final product. The extent to which you need to customize your styles depends on what you are making.

If you are developing an administration interface that will be used by a small group of people, you could do this with very little customization. However, you should always try to do some minor customizations, for example, change the primary color of your theme to match a color in the client's logo or something similar to it and make them feel more at home while using your product.

On the other hand, if you are making a public website, you need to customize your theme in order to give it a professional feel. The easiest way to give that feel to your website is applying a professional-level theme to it and tweaking it according to your needs.

Finding a suitable theme

There are a lot of themes available for Bootstrap, both free and paid. In general, there is not much of a difference in the quality between paid and free themes, but if you go for a paid theme, there are many more options to choose from.

There are many websites that offer Bootstrap themes. The following are some of the popular ones:

- `http://bootswatch.com` (free)
- `http://startbootstrap.com` (free)
- `http://jobpixels.com` (free)
- `http://bootstrappage.com` (free and paid)
- `http://wrapbootstrap.com` (paid)
- `http://themes.walkingpixels.com` (paid)
- `http://themeforest.net` (paid)

You may be wondering why someone would buy a theme instead of just making their own. The reason is simple yet easily overlooked. It is not that easy to build a professional Bootstrap theme, especially not a responsive one. There is a great deal that you need to know about Bootstrap and LESS in order to do so. Do not worry; you will soon build your own theme and see how challenging it can be.

In order to make things easier, just choose Journal (`http://bootswatch.com/journal/`), a modern newspaper-like theme, for your first Bootstrap app. This way, you do not need to browse through thousands of themes and try to decide which one to go with. Go ahead and download Journal from Bootswatch; for now, you only need the `bootstrap.min.css` file. Next, you will add your newly downloaded theme to the project that we started in the previous chapter.

Applying the theme

In the previous chapter, you created a very basic Bootstrap project using the default build of Bootstrap. That project did not do much, so let us add some more HTML to it in order to see what your new theme does to it. Replace the contents in `index.html` with the following:

```html
<!DOCTYPE html>
<html>
  <head>
    <title>A simple blog </title>
    <meta name="viewport" content="width=device-width, initial-scale=1.0">
    <link href="css/bootstrap.min.css" rel="stylesheet">
    <link href="css/custom.css" rel="stylesheet">
  </head>
  <body>
    <nav class="navbar navbar-default" role="navigation">
      <div class="container">
        <div class="navbar-header">
          <button type="button" class="navbar-toggle" data-toggle="collapse" data-target="#bs-example-navbar-collapse-1">
            <span class="sr-only">Toggle navigation</span>
            <span class="icon-bar"></span>
            <span class="icon-bar"></span>
            <span class="icon-bar"></span>
          </button>
          <a class="navbar-brand" href="#">Blog</a>
        </div>
        <div class="collapse navbar-collapse" id="bs-example-navbar-collapse-1">
          <ul class="nav navbar-nav">
            <li class="active"><a href="#">Home</a></li>
            <li><a href="#">Archive</a></li>
            <li><a href="#">About</a></li>
            <li><a href="#">Contact</a></li>
          </ul>
        </div>
```

```html
      </div>
    </nav>
    <div class="container">
      <div class="content">
        <div class="jumbotron">
          <div class="container">
            <h1>A simple blog</h1>
          </div>
        </div>
        <article>
          <header>
            <h2>Extending Bootstrap</h2>
            <p><time pubdate="pubdate">1/12/2012 3:36 PM</time> &middot; <a href="#">Blogger</a></p>
          </header>
          <p>Recently I stumbled on a book on extending Twitter Bootstrap and it really...</p>
          <p class="read-more"><a href="#">Read more &raquo;</a></p>
          <footer>
            <ul class="list-inline">
              <li><a href="#" class="label label-primary">Bootstrap</a></li>
              <li><a href="#" class="label label-primary">CSS</a></li>
              <li><a href="#" class="label label-primary">LESS</a></li>
              <li><a href="#" class="label label-primary">JavaScript</a></li>
              <li><a href="#" class="label label-primary">Grunt</a></li>
            </ul>
          </footer>
        </article>
      </div>
    </div>
    <script src="https://code.jquery.com/jquery.js"></script>
    <script src="//netdna.bootstrapcdn.com/bootstrap/3.1.1/js/bootstrap.min.js"></script>
  </body>
</html>
```

Applying a Custom Theme

Reload your browser, and your project should now look something like the following screenshot:

Now it is time to apply the theme that you downloaded. Grab the file that you downloaded from Bootswatch and replace your `bootstrap.min.css` file with it. If you now reload your browser, you will notice that your page looks a bit different in terms of font and color, as shown in the following screenshot:

As you may have noticed, the page looks a bit different after you applied the theme; this is only scratching the surface with customizing Bootstrap. Next, you will learn how to perform some simple customizations in your newly applied theme.

Customizing your theme

The easiest way to customize a theme is to override its styles. It is preferable that you use Google Chrome because of its outstanding Developer Tools, but you are free to use any tool that you feel comfortable with. However, the examples in this book use Chrome developer tools, so it may be easier to follow if you use this as well. Perform the following steps to customize your theme:

1. Start by opening your browser and toggle the developer tools by pressing *F12* on Windows or *Alt + Command + C* on OS X. You should see something like the following screenshot:

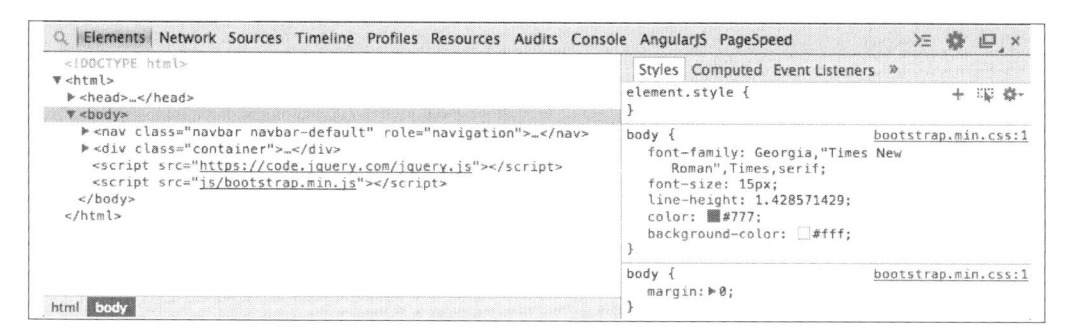

2. Before you start overriding styles, let us take a quick look at the developer tools. You only need to use the **Elements** tab that consists of the DOM structure (on the left) and the styles (on the right). In order to override a specific style, you need to find its current definition. This is where the developer tools come in. While this might seem unnecessary to some, it is very important that you look up the definition for the style that you are overriding in order to make sure that your selector actually overrides the style wanted.

   To override styles, you should create a new style sheet named `custom.css` and include it directly after `bootstrap.min.css` in `index.html`; this is shown in the following code snippet:

   ```
   <head>
     <title>A simple blog &middot;
     </title>
     <meta name="viewport" content="width=device-width,
       initial-scale=1.0">
     <link href="css/bootstrap.min.css" rel="stylesheet">
     <link href="css/custom.css" rel="stylesheet">
   </head>
   ```

3. First, you could get rid of those rounded corners; they are a bit outdated anyway. Use the Inspect tool in the developer tools to find `jumbotron`.

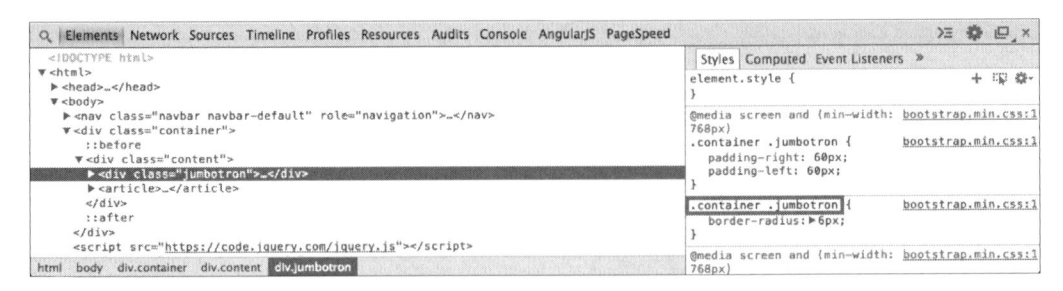

   Sometimes, you may have to scroll down quite a bit in order to find the style that you want to override.

4. As you can see from the preceding screenshot, the jumbotron styles are defined with a `.container .jumbotron` selector in `bootstrap.min.css`. To remove its rounded corners, you need to define a new style using the same selector in `custom.css`:

   ```
   .container .jumbotron {
     border-radius: 0;
   }
   ```

5. While you are at it, you might as well remove the rounded corners from the labels in the following manner:

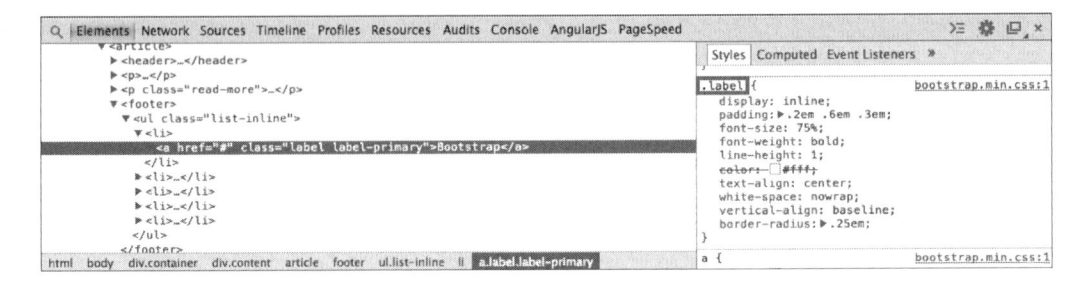

   Note that the labels are defined with a `.label` selector, so you need to define the following style in `custom.css` to remove the rounded corners:

   ```
   .label {
     border-radius: 0;
   }
   ```

6. Now that you have done some minor customizations, it is time you do some major ones. Let us change the primary color from the light red color that the Journal theme uses to one of my favorite colors, `#bada55`, which is a lime green color. Use the same technique to find the selector for each element.

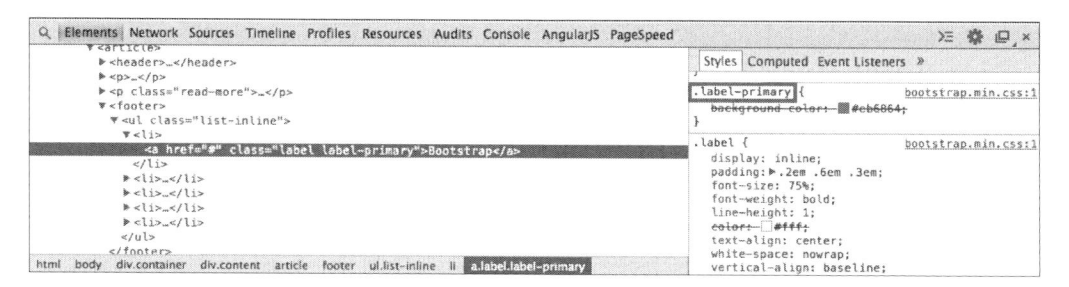

Label colors are defined with a `.label-primary` selector, so add the following code to `custom.css`:

```
.label-primary {
  background-color: #bada55;
}
```

> Always use the same property when you override styles, for example, use `background-color` instead of its shortcut `background` because `background-color` takes precedence over `background`.

7. The labels in the example are links, so you will need to override some more styles or they will still turn red when hovered or focused on. Use the Toggle Element State tool, which can be found in the top-right corner of the **Styles** tab, to emulate a state in order to see the styles for it:

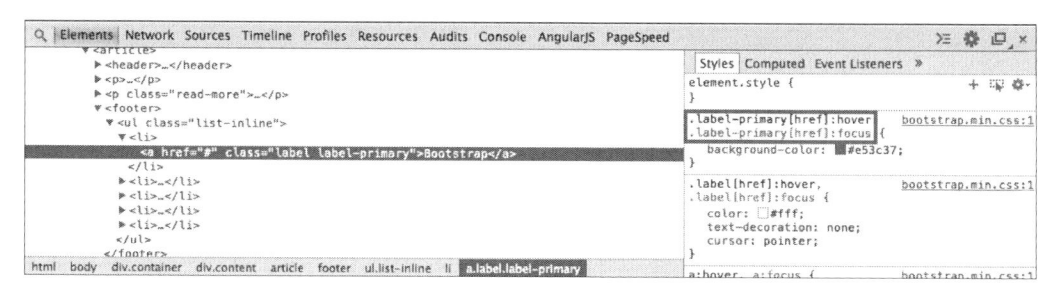

[19]

Applying a Custom Theme

8. You need to add the following additional styles to `custom.css`:

   ```
   .label-primary[href]:hover,
   .label-primary[href]:focus {
       background-color: #bada55;
   }
   ```

9. There is still one more thing left to do, that is, change the color of the links. Link styles are usually defined at a global level, so there is no specific class that you need to use as a selector. However, in order to change the behavior of all the states, you need to use some additional rules. Add the following code to `custom.css`:

   ```
   a,
   a:active,
   a:focus,
   a:hover,
   a:visited {
     color: #bada55;
   }
   ```

10. Now, if you now reload the page, it should look something like the following screenshot:

![A simple blog screenshot showing BLOG navigation with Home, Archive, About, Contact links, a header "A simple blog", and a post titled "Extending Bootstrap" dated 1/12/2012 3:36 PM with lorem ipsum text and tags.]

This is just a fraction of what you can do when it comes to customization of Bootstrap themes through overriding styles in CSS. Feel free to use your imagination to customize the example further. Next, you will learn some best practices to bear in mind when customizing Bootstrap themes through CSS.

Best practices

There are a lot of best practices when it comes to customizing Bootstrap themes. In order to avoid the most common mistakes that developers make, the following is a list of the most important things to be kept in mind:

- **Use similar selectors when overriding styles**: You should always use the exact same selector when you are overriding a style to make sure that the selector is efficient enough. You can use tools (for example, Chrome development tools) to find the correct selectors.

- **Make sure that the files are included in the correct order**: Remember that you always need to include your overrides after the original styles, otherwise they will not work.

- **Do not modify the source files**: It is considered bad practice to modify the source files directly because it makes both maintaining your customizations and upgrading the source files difficult, sometimes even impossible. There are no exceptions in this case.

- **Do not use !important unless absolutely necessary**: You should avoid using !important in your styles because it usually means that your selector is either wrong or not efficient enough. However, there are some rare cases where you need to use !important in order to override a style. If you do, try to learn why you have to use it before doing so. A good article on this topic can be found at http://coding.smashingmagazine.com/2010/11/02/the-important-css-declaration-how-and-when-to-use-it/.

- **Use classes to style elements and IDs for binding JavaScript functionalities**: This way, you can distinguish between the attributes used to define styles for an element and the attributes that are used to identify it through JavaScript.

- **Learn how Cascade works**: You can improve your styles quite a bit if you understand how CSS Cascade works, that is, how browsers parse your styles and determine which styles are more significant than others. A good article on this topic can be found at http://coding.smashingmagazine.com/2010/04/07/css-specificity-and-inheritance/.

Summary

You now know the basics of customizing Bootstrap and also know why you should always theme your Bootstrap projects at least to some extent.

In this chapter, you have learned when you should use a custom theme, where you can find a suitable theme, and how you can apply it to your project. In addition to this, you have also learned how to customize Bootstrap themes through CSS along with some best practices to consider when overriding styles.

In the next chapter, you will create your own build of Bootstrap and learn how to minimize your codebase by choosing only what you need from Bootstrap.

3
Creating Your Own Build

In this chapter, you will learn when you should create your own build of Bootstrap, how to do it using the custom tool on the Bootstrap website, and how to minimize the size of your build by removing the components that you do not need. In the previous chapter, you learned about custom themes, but now it is time to leave those themes behind and step up the game by customizing Bootstrap using more advanced methods.

Need to customize Bootstrap

When you use Bootstrap to build a professional web application, it is important that you create your own custom build. Some argue that CSS frameworks should not be used in business applications, but modern frameworks such as Bootstrap provide very good building blocks to build your own styles from the ground up. The following are some advantages of using Bootstrap that you should consider while deciding whether to use Bootstrap or write the equivalent code yourself:

- **Community driven**: Bootstrap is one of the most popular projects on GitHub and has been forked more than 20,000 times. A lot of developers all over the world have contributed to Bootstrap over the years to make it what it is today.
- **Fully customizable**: Bootstrap is built with customization in mind. You can choose exactly what you need, so if you only want to use the grid or some of the components, you can leave out everything else. If you later decide that you need something more in Bootstrap, you can include it.
- **Widely used**: It is relatively easier to find developers who are familiar with Bootstrap than teach new developers how your proprietary CSS framework works, which could be a bit more challenging.

- **100 percent unit tested**: Every great project includes unit tests for its code and so does Bootstrap. It is easy to contribute to Bootstrap because you can easily test your changes by running tests to see whether you have broken something. Unit tests also ensure the stability of the project, at least to some extent.
- **No need to reinvent the wheel**: It is not easy to write your own CSS framework with responsive capabilities. Fortunately, Bootstrap comes with a state-of-the-art responsive grid and is both easy to customize and extend. In most cases, you are better off with Bootstrap than your own framework.

Generating a custom build

Bootstrap is written in LESS, a dynamic style sheet language that compiles into CSS. LESS allows for many features that traditional style sheets do not, such as defining variables and mixins (functions), nesting of rules, and built-in methods. You will learn more about LESS in the next chapter. Bootstrap is mainly developed for customization, so it makes heavy use of LESS features to allow for advanced customizations.

The easiest way to create a custom build is to use the customization tool on the project website. With this tool, you can set custom colors and fonts and customize the grid and components, as well as choose which parts of Bootstrap to include in your build. The tool uses LESS to create the build and compiles it into CSS before sending it your way.

Now it is time to learn a bit more about the custom tool and use it to create your first custom Bootstrap build. Open your web browser and navigate to `http://getbootstrap.com/customize`. As you probably noticed, the tool is divided into four sections: **LESS components**, **jQuery plugins**, **LESS variables**, and **Download**. The first two sections allow you to choose which parts of Bootstrap you want to include in your build, and the third section lets you customize colors, fonts, paddings, and so on to suit your needs.

The fourth section allows you to download your custom version of Bootstrap, which can be seen in the following screenshot:

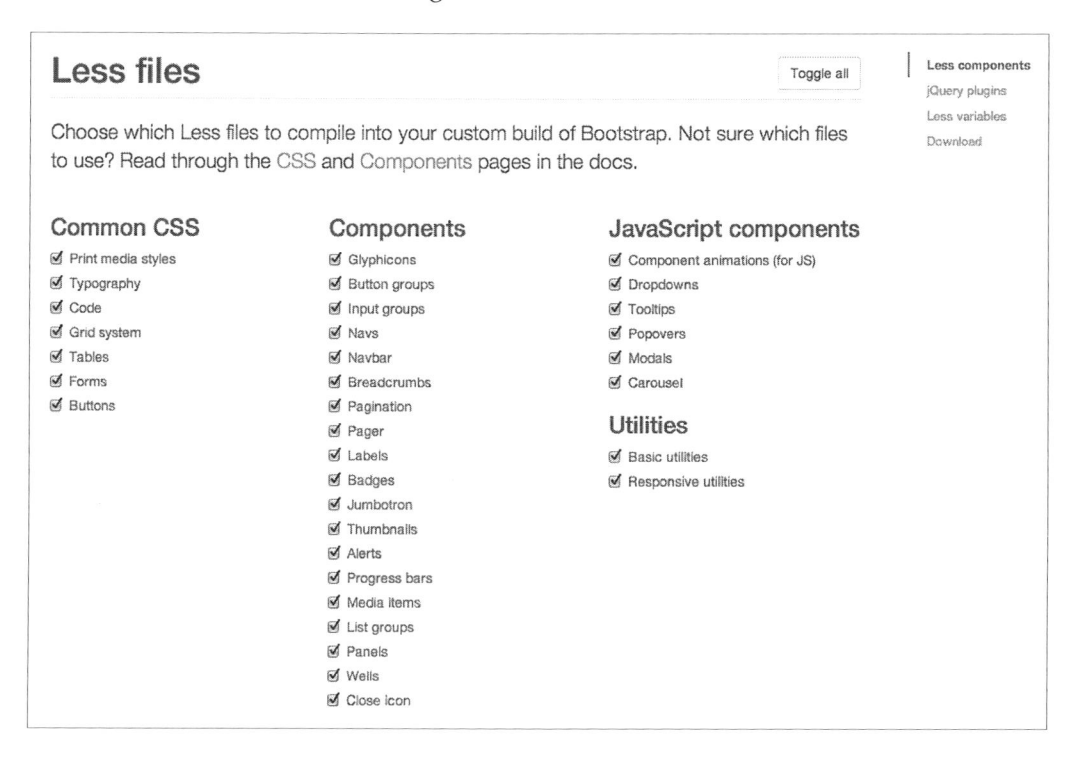

Less files

Choose which Less files to compile into your custom build of Bootstrap. Not sure which files to use? Read through the CSS and Components pages in the docs.

Common CSS
- ☑ Print media styles
- ☑ Typography
- ☑ Code
- ☑ Grid system
- ☑ Tables
- ☑ Forms
- ☑ Buttons

Components
- ☑ Glyphicons
- ☑ Button groups
- ☑ Input groups
- ☑ Navs
- ☑ Navbar
- ☑ Breadcrumbs
- ☑ Pagination
- ☑ Pager
- ☑ Labels
- ☑ Badges
- ☑ Jumbotron
- ☑ Thumbnails
- ☑ Alerts
- ☑ Progress bars
- ☑ Media items
- ☑ List groups
- ☑ Panels
- ☑ Wells
- ☑ Close icon

JavaScript components
- ☑ Component animations (for JS)
- ☑ Dropdowns
- ☑ Tooltips
- ☑ Popovers
- ☑ Modals
- ☑ Carousel

Utilities
- ☑ Basic utilities
- ☑ Responsive utilities

For your first build, you can leave the selections under the **LESS components** and **jQuery plugins** sections as they are and skip ahead to the **LESS variables** section. To see how useful the tool can be, you will choose exactly the same customizations as you did in the previous chapter. If you have already forgotten those customizations, do not worry, we will go over them again.

Creating Your Own Build

In the previous chapter, you changed the primary color from the default blue color to a lime green color. You can do the same with the tool; scroll down to **Color system**, which can be found under **Basics** and change the value in the `@brand-primary` field to `#bada55` as shown in the following screenshot:

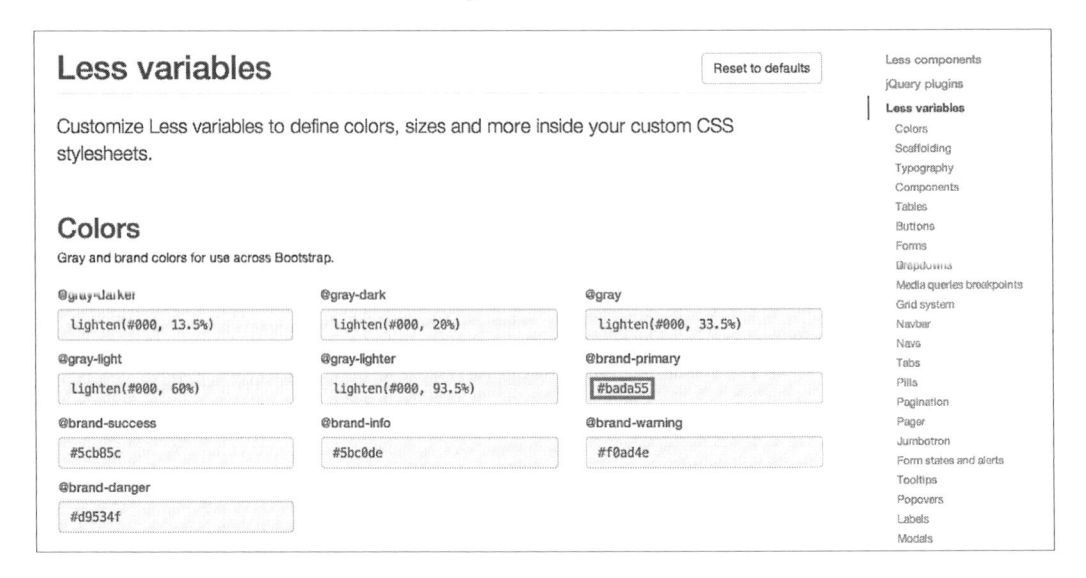

As you may remember, you also removed the rounded corners from some elements. Unfortunately, the tool is a bit limited and allows you to customize the border radius only for a few elements, so you will have to skip this customization for now. We will get back to removing the rounded corners later.

Now you are ready to download your first custom build of Bootstrap; scroll down and hit the download button at the bottom of the page as shown in the following screenshot. When the build is ready, you will receive it as a ZIP file that contains three folders: `css`, `fonts`, and `js` and a `config.json` file that is used by the tool. Open the `css` folder and replace `bootstrap.min.css` in your project with the one you just downloaded from the build.

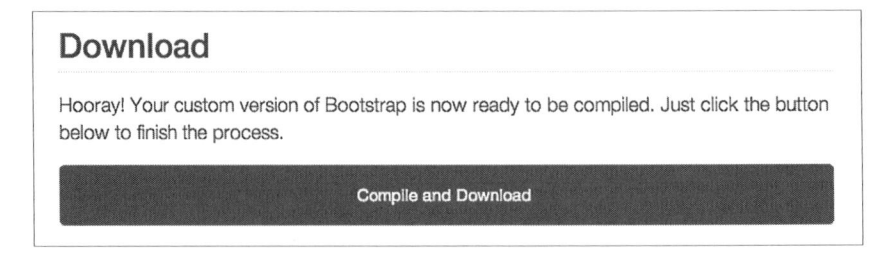

[26]

Alternatively, we can get rid of the color styles in the `custom.css` file, so open it and remove everything else other than the following styles:

```
.container .jumbotron {
  border-radius: 0;
}
.label {
  border-radius: 0;
}
```

If you now reload the project, it should look exactly like it did at the end of *Chapter 2, Applying a Custom Theme*, as shown in the following screenshot:

Keeping only what you need

It is always a good idea to minimize the code base in your libraries. So, next you will learn how to include only the parts of Bootstrap that you absolutely need. As you have already seen, the custom tool lets you choose which LESS components and jQuery plugins to include in your build. If you look at your `bootstrap.min.css` file, which is your minified version of Bootstrap, you can see that it is 100 KB in size. Now, let us see how much size is reduced when we leave out everything that you do not need.

Creating Your Own Build

Go back to the tool and click on **Toggle all** in the **LESS components** section to remove all the selections and then check the items as shown the following screenshot. Scroll down to the bottom of the page and hit the download button.

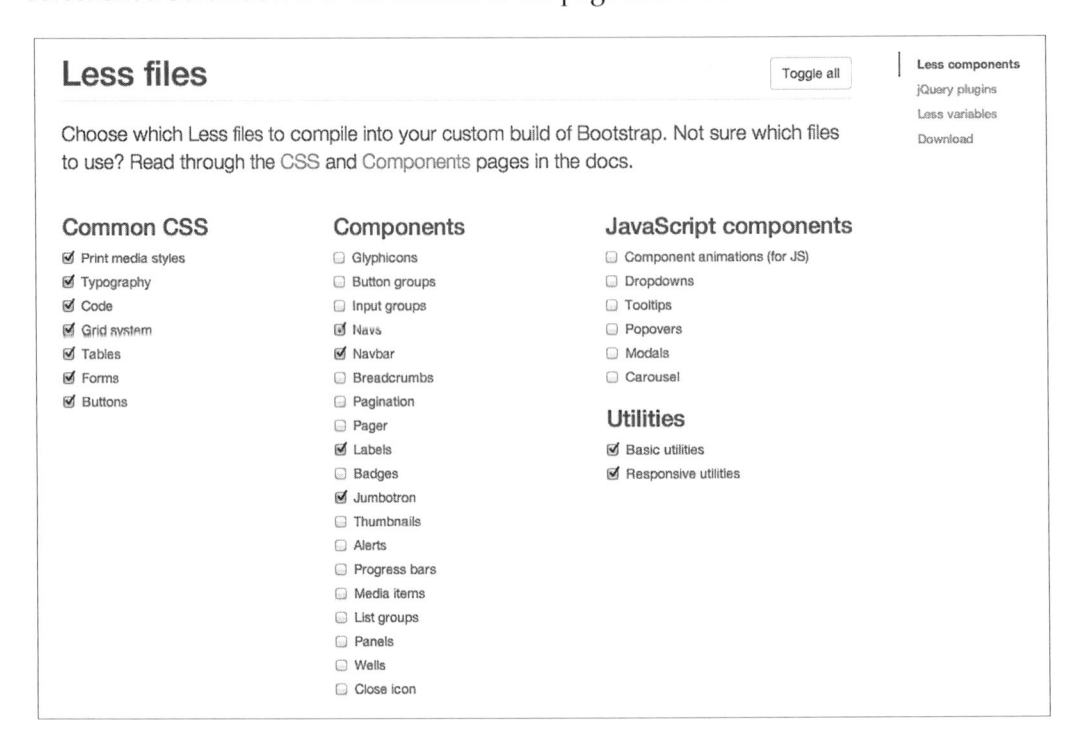

Less files

Choose which Less files to compile into your custom build of Bootstrap. Not sure which files to use? Read through the CSS and Components pages in the docs.

Toggle all

Less components
jQuery plugins
Less variables
Download

Common CSS
- ☑ Print media styles
- ☑ Typography
- ☑ Code
- ☑ Grid system
- ☑ Tables
- ☑ Forms
- ☑ Buttons

Components
- ☐ Glyphicons
- ☐ Button groups
- ☐ Input groups
- ☑ Navs
- ☑ Navbar
- ☐ Breadcrumbs
- ☐ Pagination
- ☐ Pager
- ☑ Labels
- ☐ Badges
- ☑ Jumbotron
- ☐ Thumbnails
- ☐ Alerts
- ☐ Progress bars
- ☐ Media items
- ☐ List groups
- ☐ Panels
- ☐ Wells
- ☐ Close icon

JavaScript components
- ☐ Component animations (for JS)
- ☐ Dropdowns
- ☐ Tooltips
- ☐ Popovers
- ☐ Modals
- ☐ Carousel

Utilities
- ☑ Basic utilities
- ☑ Responsive utilities

If you now take a look at `bootstrap.min.css`, you will notice that it is around 58 KB, which is almost half the size of what it used to be. While it might not seem like much, each KB counts when people are downloading static files from your web server, so always remember to leave out the parts of Bootstrap that you do not need.

> Even though the custom tool has its limits, it is a very powerful tool, so feel free to experiment all you want.

Summary

Now you have learned why you should customize Bootstrap, how to generate your custom build, and how to leave out the parts of Bootstrap that you do not need.

In this chapter, you customized Bootstrap by creating your own build and replaced Bootstrap in your project with the one from your new build to reduce its size.

In the next chapter, things will get exciting when you learn the basics of LESS and start customizing Bootstrap on a whole new level. Forget about traditional CSS, with LESS you can do so much more!

4
LESS is More

In this chapter, you will learn the basics of LESS and understand why it is better than traditional CSS. You will compile your own build from the Bootstrap source, replace the CSS in your project with LESS, and learn to customize Bootstrap with LESS and use its mixins.

Why use LESS?

LESS is a dynamic style sheet language that is compiled into CSS. The compiler itself is written in JavaScript and is quite fast compared to its alternatives, SASS and Stylus.

LESS comes with a wide range of useful features that are not available in traditional CSS, such as variables, mixins, nested rules, functions, and operators. Let's face it. Writing CSS is tiresome and includes a lot of repetition. When you write your styles in LESS instead of traditional CSS, you can use the following features to improve your styles:

- **Variables**: Variables have always been missing from CSS. By using LESS, you can define your own variables to make your styles more dynamic and configurable.
- **Mixins**: Mixins are named methods that can be used over and over again to repeat an operation. They can also take arguments and support default values for these arguments. Mixins are a great way to get rid of browser-specific CSS prefixes.
- **Nested rules**: Instead of writing the same selector over and over again, you can use a parent selector and declare your rules for child elements within that rule to reduce the need for repetition.

- **Functions**: LESS includes a number of color functions, for example, darken and lighten functions that ease working with colors. You can also switch between different color schemes, such as HSL and RGB, with ease.
- **Operators**: With LESS, you can perform simple mathematical operations to calculate widths, margins, paddings, and so on. This comes really handy when you want to customize a grid in Bootstrap or write your own grid.

Compiling your first LESS file

The easiest way to compile LESS files is to install Node.js and use its package manager **NPM** to install RECESS. There are Node.js installers available for both OS X and Windows. In case you are running Linux, visit https://github.com/joyent/node/wiki/Installing-Node.js-via-package-manager for instructions on how to install Node.js via package managers.

Once you have Node.js up and running, you can run the npm command to install RECESS, which is a CSS hinter written by Jacob Thornton himself. It is the only compiler officially supported by Bootstrap, and it can compile LESS into CSS among other things. You can install RECESS by running the following command:

```
npm install -g recess
```

This will install RECESS globally on your system. Now that you have RECESS installed, its time to create your first LESS file. Create a new folder named `less` in the project root and then create a file named `styles.less` in it. Add the following code to your newly created file:

```
@font-family: Arial;
@text-color: red;
body {
  font-family: @font-family;
  color: @text-color;
}
```

To compile the file, navigate to your project root and run the following command:

```
recess styles.less --compile > styles.css
```

> The latest version of Bootstrap, v3.1.x, will not compile using RECESS anymore since they moved to use grunt-contrib-less for compilation.

This will compile the code in your `styles.less` file and place the result in a file named `styles.css`. If you look into the file created by the compiler, you should see the following:

```
body {
  font-family: Arial;
  color: #ff0000;
}
```

> You can also compress the style by running RECESS with the `--compress` option in the following way:
>
> **`recess styles.less --compress > styles.css`**
>
> This will produce the following output:
>
> `body{font-family:Arial;color:#f00}`

To learn more about what RECESS can do for you, visit the project website at https://github.com/twitter/recess.

Building Bootstrap from the source

Before you can build Bootstrap from source, you need to download the source from the project website. Once you have downloaded the source and opened the package, you will see that the source package contains a large number of directories and files. You need to perform the following steps in order to build Bootstrap from source:

1. Unzip the package you downloaded in a location where you can easily find it. Create a new folder named `less` for the LESS files in your project and a `bootstrap` folder within that folder. Copy the contents of the `less` folder from the files that you just unzipped, and place it in the `bootstrap` folder, which is inside the `less` folder.

2. Create an entry LESS file called `main.less` under the `less` directory and add the following content:

   `@import "bootstrap/bootstrap";`

   This will include the Bootstrap entry file, which includes all of the Bootstrap features and produces exactly the same result as when you use the default `bootstrap.css` file.

3. Run the following command in the root of your project to use RECESS to compile your styles:

   `recess less/main.less --compile > css/main.css`

This will compile your LESS file, including all of the Bootstrap features into a `main.css` file under the `css` directory in your project.

4. Open `index.html` and remove the following lines:

   ```
   <link href="css/bootstrap.min.css" rel="stylesheet"/>
   <link href="css/custom.css" rel="stylesheet"/>
   ```

5. Add the following line instead:

   ```
   <link href="main.css" rel="stylesheet"/>
   ```

   Now, when you reload the project, it will look exactly like it did before you added any customizations, and it now uses your own custom build of Bootstrap that you just compiled with RECESS, as shown in the following screenshot:

Next, you will restore the customizations that you already created in *Chapter 2*, *Applying a Custom Theme*, and add a few new ones. Now that you are using LESS, it will be easier to apply customizations to your project.

Customizing variables

The easiest way to customize Bootstrap through LESS is to customize its variables. To do this, you need to perform the following few modifications to your project:

1. Create a new LESS file named `custom-variables.less` in the `less` directory. Open `main.less` and add the following line to import the new file:

   ```
   @import "custom-variables";
   ```

   You can now override Bootstrap variables easily by redeclaring them in `custom-variables.less`, and Bootstrap will use the overridden values instead of the defaults when it is compiled into CSS.

2. Open `custom-variables.less` and add the following line:

   ```
   @brand-color: #bada55;
   ```

   This will override the primary color in Bootstrap with the same greenish color that you used in the previous chapter. As you can see, instead of overriding a lot of rules, we simply need to change the value of a single LESS variable in order to apply the customization to all of the elements that use the primary color across Bootstrap. It is also worth mentioning that back when you used CSS, you only added rules for those components that were used on the page. It would take a lot more rules to override all of the elements to use your own primary color.

3. It is time to get rid of your `custom.css` and use LESS to apply the customizations instead. Create a new LESS file named `custom-theme.less` in the `less` directory and copy the following content from `custom.css` to it, after which you can delete `custom.css`:

   ```
   .container .jumbotron {
     border-radius: 0;
   }
   .label {
     border-radius: 0;
   }
   ```

4. Now, add the following line to import your theme at the end of `main.less`:

   ```
   @import "custom-theme";
   ```

   When you now recompile `main.less` and reload your project, you will see that you have reapplied all the customizations to it from earlier, as shown in the following screenshot:

LESS is More

5. Now that you are at it, you could add some more advanced customizations to your project. Let us start by customizing the colors a bit. Add the following to `custom-variables.less`:

   ```
   @navbar-default-bg:                   darken(@brand-primary, 10%);
   @navbar-default-brand-hover-color:    #fff;
   @navbar-default-link-color:           #fff;
   @navbar-default-link-active-color:    lighten(@brand-primary, 25%);
   @navbar-default-link-active-bg:       darken(@brand-primary, 20%);

   @jumbotron-bg:                        lighten(@brand-primary, 30%);
   ```

6. Save the file, compile your styles, and reload your project. You should see the following screenshot:

7. Let us step up the game a bit by adding some more HTML to the page. Replace the contents of your outermost div element `.container div` with the following code:

   ```
   <div class="row">
     <div class="content">
       <div class="jumbotron">
         <div class="container">
           <h1>A simple blog</h1>
         </div>
       </div>
       <article>
   ```

```html
<header>
  <h2>Extending Bootstrap</h2>
  <p><time pubdate="pubdate">1/12/2012 3:36 PM</time>
    &middot; <a href="#">Blogger</a></p>
</header>
<p>Recently I stumbled on a book on extending Twitter
  Bootstrap and it really ...</p>
<p class="read-more"><a href="#">Read more
  &raquo;</a></p>
<footer>
  <ul class="list-inline">
    <li><a href="#" class="label label-
      primary">Bootstrap</a></li>
    <li><a href="#" class="label label-
      primary">CSS</a></li>
    <li><a href="#" class="label label-
      primary">LESS</a></li>
    <li><a href="#" class="label label-
      primary">JavaScript</a></li>
    <li><a href="#" class="label label-
      primary">Grunt</a></li>
  </ul>
</footer>
      </article>
    </div>
    <aside class="sidebar">
      <img class="sidebar-avatar" src="http://
        lorempixel.com/400/400/cats" alt="Avatar"/>
      <p class="sidebar-bio">Christoffer is a web developer
        that Lorem ipsum dolor sit amet, consectetur
        adipisicing elit. Asperiores, maxime, neque?
        Assumenda at commodi et eum illum, incidunt ipsa
        laborum molestias, necessitatibus numquam quod
        ratione sint vero. Amet, facilis iusto. </p>
    </aside>
</div>
```

8. Add the following style to `custom-theme.less`:

```less
.content {
  .make-md-column(9);

  article {
    margin-bottom: 40px;
  }
}
```

LESS is More

```
.sidebar {
  .make-md-column(3);
}
.sidebar-avatar {
  display: block;
  margin-bottom: 20px;
  max-width: 100%;
}
.sidebar-bio {
  color: @gray;
}
```

Now if you compile your styles and reload the project, it should look something like the following:

Let us walk through what you just did. You added some HTML and CSS for the sidebar and used two mixins to turn the .content and .sidebar elements into grid elements. A grid in Bootstrap consists of 12 columns by default, so adding .make-md-column(9) to .content makes it span three quarters; leaving one quarter for the sidebar and adding .make-md-column(3) to .sidebar makes use of the rest of the space.

> In case you have not noticed, your project is fully responsive. You can try resizing your browser window to see how the grid responds when the window size is adjusted.

Bootstrap comes with a large collection of useful mixins, such as gradients, CSS3 properties, various components, and grid, for various purposes. All of these are great once you learn how to use them; they are listed as follows:

- **Gradients**: Bootstrap supports many kinds of gradients, such as horizontal, vertical, directional, radial, striped, and both horizontal and vertical gradients with three colors. When you use Bootstrap mixins for gradients, you do not need to worry about browser compatibility because Bootstrap adds all browser-specific rules automatically, even for Internet Explorer 8.
- **CSS3 properties**: Bootstrap comes with mixins for the most commonly used CSS properties, such as box-shadow, transition, transform (rotate, scale, and translate), perspective, animation, backface-visibility, box-sizing, use-select, content-columns, and hyphens. These CSS3 mixins also work across all browsers.
- **Component**: Component-specific mixins are handy when you want to perform more advanced customizations to Bootstrap components. Components such as panels, alerts, tables, list groups, buttons, labels, the navbar, and progress bar have their own mixins in Bootstrap.
- **Grid**: Bootstrap uses mixins to build its grid. It is considered as a good practice to avoid vendor-specific classes such as `.col-md-6` in your HTML in order to allow for the separation of structure and layout. You can achieve this by adding custom classes to your elements and using mixins such as `.make-md-column(6)` to make them act like grid columns instead.

Summary

You have now learned the basics of LESS—why you should use it, how to build Bootstrap from source, and how to customize it using LESS.

In this chapter, you customized Bootstrap using LESS by compiling it from source and applying your modifications by customizing variables and using Bootstrap mixins.

In the next chapter, you will learn about Grunt, a task runner for Node.js that can do many things, such as watch your LESS files for change, compile your LESS file, and even automatically reload the browser after it has compiled your LESS file.

5
Compiling Your Styles with Grunt

In this chapter, you will be introduced to Grunt, a task-runner for Node.js. You will learn how to install Grunt, how to use it to compile your LESS files, how to configure the `watch` plugin to watch your files for changes, and how to set up automatic reloading in your browser.

Why build LESS files with Grunt?

So far, you have compiled your LESS files by hand with Twitter's RECESS. This works fine, but there is a far more efficient way to compile your styles. You can use Grunt and its plugins to automate the compilation of your styles. The following are the benefits of Grunt:

- **Easy to install and configure**: Grunt is easily installed through **Node Package Manager** (**NPM**) and its configuration file is a JavaScript file, so it is easy to configure it to do more when necessary.

- **A single configuration for the whole team**: You can add the Grunt configuration file, `Gruntfile` (and the NPM dependency manifest, `package.json`), to your repository to share your Grunt stack with everyone on your development team and reduce the required amount of configuration for everyone.

- **Automatic compilation**: With Grunt and its Watch plugin, you can set up watching for your LESS files and make Grunt run the compilation task when it notices a change in the file.

- **Live reloading**: Grunt's Watch plugin now also features a built-in live-reload server (since v5.x), so you can even make your browser refresh the page when Grunt has recompiled your styles.
- **Can be used for all kind of tasks**: Grunt is a task runner with over 2000 plugins written by talented people. It can be used for many other things than just the compilation of LESS; for example, minifying of scripts, running tests, optimizing of images, and much more.

Using Grunt to build your project

Now that you know why you should use Grunt, it is time to install it. Let us start with a very simple configuration and expand from there. To do so, perform the following steps:

1. You should already have Node.js installed, so you can use NPM to install Grunt by running the following command in your project root (if not, refer to *Chapter 4*, *LESS is More*, for instructions on installing Node.js):

   ```
   sudo npm install -g grunt-cli
   ```

2. This will install the Grunt command-line utility globally on your system. In case you already have it installed, you can skip this step.

3. Run the following commands to initialize NPM for your project and install Grunt:

   ```
   sudo npm init
   npm install grunt --save-dev
   ```

   > Appending the `--save-dev` flag to the command adds the plugin as a project development dependency in `package.json` (if you have one).

4. Next, you need to install the LESS plugin to be able to compile your styles. You can do that by running the following command in your project root:

   ```
   npm install grunt-contrib-less --save-dev
   ```

5. You have installed everything that you need for now. So, you are ready to create your first Grunt configuration file. Create a new JavaScript file called `Gruntfile.js` in your project folder and add the following contents:

   ```
   module.exports = function (grunt) {
     // Grunt configuration
     grunt.initConfig({
   ```

```
    less: {
      app: {
        files: {"less/main.less": "css/main.css"}
      }
    }
  });

  // Load plugins
  grunt.loadNpmTasks("grunt-contrib-less");
};
```

6. This configuration file consists of two sections: the actual configuration and loading of a single task. The `initConfig` method allows you to pass parameters to Grunt plugins. In this example, we define a subtask for the `less` plugin called `app`, which compiles the styles for your application.

> For more information on the LESS plugin, refer to its documentation at https://github.com/gruntjs/grunt-contrib-less.

7. Now that you have a configuration file for Grunt, you can use it to compile your styles by running the following command:

   grunt less:app

   This will do pretty much the same as running RECESS to compile your styles except now that you are using Grunt, you can automate the compilation. That is what you will do next.

Now that you have Grunt up and running, you can start unlocking some of its true power and configure it to automatically compile your styles when it notices that they have changed. To do so, perform the following steps:

1. First you need to install the `watch` plugin by running the following command:

   npm install grunt-contrib-watch --save-dev

2. Replace the contents of `Gruntfile` with the following:

```
module.exports = function (grunt) {
  // Grunt configuration
  grunt.initConfig({
    less: {
      app: {
```

```
            files: {"css/main.css": "less/main.less"}
          }
        },
        watch: {
          styles: {
            files: ["less/**/*.less"],
            tasks: ["less:app"],
            options: {spawn: false}
          }
        }
      });

      // Load plugins
      grunt.loadNpmTasks("grunt-contrib-less");
      grunt.loadNpmTasks("grunt-contrib-watch"),
    };
```

3. The new configuration does not differ much from the previous one, but it registers and adds a subtask for the `watch` plugin called `styles`, which watches all LESS files recursively within the `less` directory and runs the `less:app` subtask if it notices a change.

> Setting the `spawn` option to `false` prevents the `watch` plugin from running its tasks in child processes, which will speed up the reaction time of the plugin considerably. It will also allow all other tasks of the `watch` plugin to share the same context.
>
> For more information on the Watch plugin, refer to its documentation at https://github.com/gruntjs/grunt-contrib-watch.

4. Run the following command to make Grunt watch your LESS files:

   `grunt watch:styles`

5. When you now make a change in one of your LESS files, you should see something similar to the following output in your command prompt:

   ```
   $ grunt watch:styles
   Running "watch:styles" (watch) task
   Waiting...OK
   >> File "less/main.less" changed.
   Running "less/app" (less) task
   File css/main.css created.
   Running "watch:styles" (watch) task
   Completed in 0.648s at Thu Jan 02 2014 13:06:57 GMT+0000 (UTC) -
   Waiting...
   ```

6. As you can see, the `less:app` subtask is now automatically run when `main.less` (or any other LESS file in the `less` directory) is changed.

> If you are using Linux, you can install GNU Screen to run Grunt in the background. For more information about using GNU Screen, refer to its documentation at https://wiki.archlinux.org/index.php/GNU_Screen.

So far, you have configured Grunt to both compile and watch your LESS files. Would it not be nice if you could see the changes live in the browser as you make them? With Grunt, this is possible; it is called live reloading, which is what we will set up next.

Using Grunt for live reloading

So far you have configured Grunt to both compile and watch your LESS files. Now it is time to make it refresh your browser window when the `watch` plugin notices a change. To do so, perform the following steps:

1. Open up `Gruntfile` and add the `livereload` option to the `watch` plugin configuration with the help of the following code:

   ```
   watch: {
     styles: {
       files: ["less/**/*.less"],
       tasks: ["less:app"],
       options: {
         livereload: true,
         spawn: false
       }
     }
   }
   ```

2. This option will tell the `watch` plugin to start a live-reload server on the default port (35729).

> You can also start the live-reload server on a different port by giving the `livereload` option a numeric value instead, for example, `livereload: 1337`. This is useful if you want to run multiple live-reload servers on the same machine.

3. Next, you need open up your `index.html` file and add the following `script` tag right before the closing `body` tag:

   ```
   <script src="http://localhost:35729/livereload.js"></script>
   ```

4. This will connect your browser to your live-reload server and allow you to reload the page when you change a file that is watched.

> There are also other options for setting up live reloading, such as using browser extensions and the `Connect` plugin. For more information, refer to the **Live Reloading** section in the Watch plugin documentation at `https://github.com/gruntjs/grunt-contrib-watch`.

Now restart Grunt, navigate to your project root with your browser, change any of your LESS files, and save it. When you do so, your browser should be automatically refreshed.

Summary

You have now learned how to install Grunt and how to automate the compilation of your styles. You also learned why you should use Grunt and what you can do with it, besides compiling your LESS files.

In this chapter, you replaced RECESS with Grunt in your project and used it to compile your styles, watch your LESS files, and reload your browser when a change is made to any LESS file.

In the next chapter, you will learn to adapt Bootstrap JavaScript plugins to suit your needs. Even though the plugins might not seem that useful at first, they can be customized to do more.

6
Adapting Bootstrap JavaScript Plugins

In this chapter, you will learn how to make the most out of the jQuery plugins that come bundled with Bootstrap. You will first learn why you should go through the trouble of customizing plugins, then understand how to do the actual customization, and finally find out how to extend the plugins properly.

Why customize plugins?

There are basically two different ways to customize the Bootstrap plugins. You can either apply your own style to alter their appearance or you can extend the functionality of the plugins to make them do what you want.

Normally, it is enough to simply apply your own style to the plugins, but occasionally, you will need to extend the functionality of the plugins to produce the desired result. The following are a few advantages to consider when customizing plugins:

- **Saves time**: Customizing the existing plugins can save you an immense amount of time compared to writing your own jQuery plugins. When you use the Bootstrap plugins, you get decent base styles for the plugins that can easily be modified and you do not need to write the styles from scratch.

- **Fairly well written**: Most of the plugins that come with Bootstrap are fairly well written and can easily be extended to do more. Back when Bootstrap was new, it was quite hard to customize the plugins, and some of them even came with a few bugs. However, things have changed since then and the plugins in the latest Bootstrap 3 are production-ready.

- **Divided opinions**: Some developers say that the Bootstrap plugins are bad and should not be used for anything other than prototyping. These developers are missing out because even if they are not the best jQuery plugins, they are still quite decent and are viable options that should be considered.

Customizing plugins

Now that you know why you should customize plugins, it is time to add some customized plugins to your Bootstrap project as shown in the following steps:

1. First open `index.html` and add the following code snippet directly after the `<nav>` element at the top of the page:

   ```
   <div id="carousel" class="carousel slide" data-ride="carousel">
     <ol class="carousel-indicators">
       <li data-target="#carousel" data-slide-to="0" class="active"></li>
       <li data-target="#carousel" data-slide-to="1"></li>
       <li data-target="#carousel" data-slide-to="2"></li>
     </ol>
     <div class="carousel-inner">
       <div class="item active">
         <div class="carousel-caption">Slide 1</div>
       </div>
       <div class="item">
         <div class="carousel-caption">Slide 2</div>
       </div>
       <div class="item">
         <div class="carousel-caption">Slide 3</div>
       </div>
     </div>
     <a class="left carousel-control" href="#carousel" data-slide="prev"><span class="glyphicon glyphicon-chevron-left"></span></a>
     <a class="right carousel-control" href="#carousel" data-slide="next"><span class="glyphicon glyphicon-chevron-right"></span></a>
   </div>
   ```

2. Next, open `custom-theme.less` and add the following code snippet:

   ```
   .carousel {
     // create a new shade of @brand-primary.
     background: lighten(@brand-primary, 35%);
     max-height: 560px;
     margin: -20px 0 40px;
     width: 100%;
   }
   ```

```less
.carousel-indicators {
  bottom: -23px;
  text-align: right;

  li {
    // set width and height equal to 15px.
    .square(15px);
    background: #fff;
    border-color: @brand-primary;

    // "&" refers to the parent element (li).
    &:hover {
      border-color: lighten(@brand-primary, 10%);
    }

    &.active {
      .square(17px);
      background-color: @brand-primary;
    }
  }
}
.carousel-inner > .item {
  max-height: 560px;
 overflow: hidden;

  > img {
    margin-top: -100px;
    width: 100%;
  }
}
.carousel-caption {
  background-color: @brand-primary;
  font-size: 1.5em;
  padding: 10px;
  text-align: left;
  text-shadow: none;
}
.carousel-control {
  color: @brand-primary;
  font-size: 3em;
  opacity: 1;
  text-shadow: none;

  &:hover {
    color: lighten(@brand-primary, 10%);
  }

  &.left, &.right {
    background: none;
  }
}
```

3. Now, if you recompile your styles, you should see the result as shown in the following screenshot. Customizing the plugins is just like customizing any Bootstrap components; find out which styles you need to override and do so.

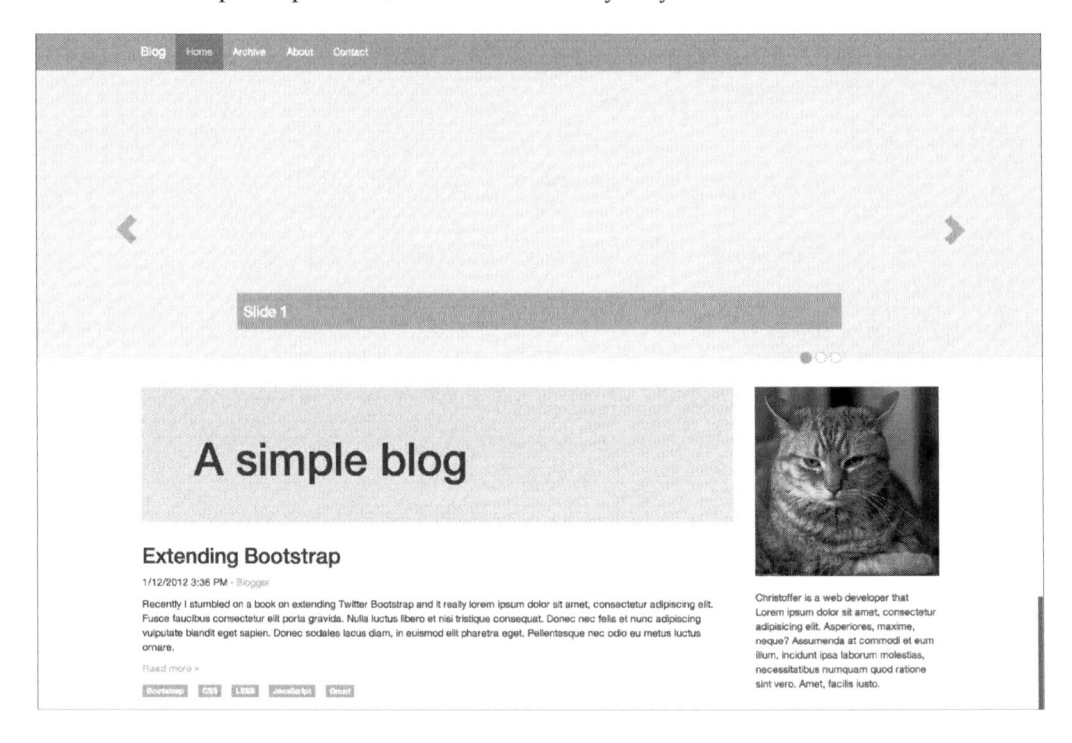

Next, we will take a look at how we can make the plugins do more.

Extending Bootstrap plugins

Sometimes, you need to extend the functionality of the Bootstrap plugins, and when you do, it is important that you know how to do it correctly. There are many ways to extend plugins. We will cover a single approach that you can implement in your projects to extend any Bootstrap plugin.

As an example, let us take a look at how you can extend the Bootstrap Modal plugin.

Create a new JavaScript file named `custom-modal.js` and add the following contents:

```
(function ($) {
  // enable ES5 strict mode
  'use strict';
```

```
  // save the original plugin
  var _parent = $.fn.modal;

  // define your own constructor
  var Modal = function(element, options) {
    _parent.Constructor.apply(this, arguments);
    // console.log calls are here just to see that our method is called.
    console.log('modal initialized');
  };

  // set custom default options
  Modal.DEFAULTS = $.extend({}, _parent.Constructor.DEFAULTS, {
    backdrop: 'static'
  });

  // extend the prototype for your plugin from the original plugin
  Modal.prototype = Object.create(_parent.Constructor.prototype);

  // define a method for easy access to parent methods
  Modal.prototype.parent = function() {
    var args = $.makeArray(arguments),
        method = args.shift();
    _parent.Constructor.prototype[method].apply(this, args)
  };

  // override the show method to demonstrate
  Modal.prototype.show = function() {
    this.parent('show');
    console.log('show called');
  };

  // override the actual jQuery plugin method
  $.fn.modal = function (option, _relatedTarget) {
    console.log('modal plugin called');
    return this.each(function () {
      var $this = $(this),
          data  = $this.data('bs.modal'),
          options = $.extend({}, Modal.DEFAULTS, $this.data(), typeof option === 'object' && option);

      if (!data) {
        $this.data('bs.modal', (data = new Modal(this, options)));
      }
```

Adapting Bootstrap JavaScript Plugins

```
      if (typeof option === 'string') {
        data[option](_relatedTarget);
      } else if (options.show) {
        data.show(_relatedTarget);
      }
    });
  };

  // override the plugin constructor
  $.fn.modal.Constructor = Modal;

  // override the plugin no-conflict method
  $.fn.modal.noConflict = function() {
    $.fn.modal = _parent;
    return this;
  };

})(jQuery);
```

Alright, that was quite a lot of code. Let us take a closer look at what the preceding code actually does:

1. To avoid polluting the global scope, everything is wrapped in an anonymous function that is invoked immediately with jQuery as its only argument. This is, nowadays, a common practice when working with JavaScript libraries:

    ```
    (function ($) {
      .....
    })(jQuery);
    ```

2. First, we save the original plugin in a variable in the following way so that we can call its methods later on:

    ```
    var _parent = $.fn.modal;
    ```

3. Then we define our own constructor, which is not absolutely necessary but is useful if we want to run custom code when the plugin is instantiated. It is defined as follows:

    ```
    var Modal = function(element, options) {
      _parent.Constructor.apply(this, arguments);
      console.log('modal initialized');
    };
    ```

4. Next, we define plugin options and their prototype by extending the default options and the prototype from the original plugin. We do it using the following code:

```
Modal.DEFAULTS = $.extend({}, _parent.Constructor.DEFAULTS,
  {
  backdrop: 'static'
});

Modal.prototype =
    Object.create(_parent.Constructor.prototype);
```

> If you want to learn more about prototypal inheritance in JavaScript, you can read about it on the Mozilla Developer Network website at https://developer.mozilla.org/en-US/docs/Web/JavaScript/Guide/Inheritance_and_the_prototype_chain.

5. Next, we define a parent method to allow us to call the methods from the original plugin easily and use that method to override the show method. This is done as follows:

```
Modal.prototype.parent = function() {
  var args = $.makeArray(arguments),
      method = args.shift();
  _parent.Constructor.prototype[method].apply(this, args)
};

Modal.prototype.show = function() {
  this.parent('show');
  console.log('show called');
};
```

6. Finally, we override the actual plugin method, its constructor, and the noConflict method with our own, as shown in the following code snippet:

```
$.fn.modal = function (option, _relatedTarget) {
  console.log('modal plugin called');
  return this.each(function () {
    var $this = $(this),
        data  = $this.data('bs.modal'),
        options = $.extend({}, Modal.DEFAULTS, $this.data(),
typeof option === 'object' && option);
```

[53]

Adapting Bootstrap JavaScript Plugins

```
      if (!data) {
        $this.data('bs.modal', (data = new Modal(this,
          options)));
      }
      if (typeof option === 'string') {
        data[option](_relatedTarget);
      } else if (options.show) {
        data.show(_relatedTarget);
      }
    });
  };

  $.fn.modal.Constructor = Modal;

  $.fn.modal.noConflict = function () {
    $.fn.modal = _parent;
    return this;
  };
```

Now, you must be wondering why we need to override the jQuery plugin and its public methods. This is because, otherwise, our custom modal plugin would only exist within our anonymous function and would never be exposed to jQuery. It's a pity that we need to redefine the plugin and its methods, but there is really no way around this.

This might seem like an awful lot of code for such a small modification, but if you really want to extend the functionality of a plugin, this is the way to go. With this approach, there is almost no limit on what you can do. Most third party libraries that extend Bootstrap work in a similar manner. You could simplify the code a bit here and there, but that would make it less extendable and therefore also harder to work with.

The key benefits of using the previously mentioned approach for extending Bootstrap plugins are as follows:

- **Extendable**: This approach is focused on extendibility. The parent method allows you to call the original methods easily. You can also override every single method in the plugin to add some extra functionality with no trouble at all.
- **Clean**: There is no need to modify the code of the actual Bootstrap plugins. Instead, you create a new plugin by extending the original one and replacing the plugin with your own. All you need to do is load your code after you load the Bootstrap JavaScript.
- **Based on best practices**: This approach is written using the best JavaScript practices. Working with JavaScript can sometimes be tricky as every task can be done in so many ways and there is never a single correct solution.

Summary

You have now learned how to customize Bootstrap plugins by adding your own styles and by defining your own jQuery plugin that extends the original plugin.

In this chapter, you included a carousel plugin in your Bootstrap project and added some custom styles to it. You also learned how to extend the functionality of the Bootstrap plugins without modifying the original plugin.

In the next chapter, you will learn how the grid in Bootstrap works and how to customize it properly. You will customize the grid in your Bootstrap project and learn more about the responsiveness.

7
Custom Grids

Nowadays, all major CSS frameworks come with a built-in grid, and Bootstrap is no exception. The grid saw major improvements when Bootstrap 3 was released, and Bootstrap became mobile first, which means that the grid starts out stacked on mobile devices and is floated through media queries on devices with wider screens. In addition to being mobile first, the grid is also fluid, which means that it uses percentages instead of pixel values.

In this chapter, you will learn to identify when you need a custom grid, how to customize the Bootstrap grid to meet your needs, as well as how to disable responsiveness in Bootstrap.

Why use a custom grid?

The grid in Bootstrap consists of 12 columns by default, but it can be customized through LESS variables. Sometimes, you will need to create a custom grid to accomplish what you want instead of writing your own grid from scratch, which takes time and can be quite complicated. You can create your grid with Bootstrap or even use the grid in Bootstrap if necessary.

There are many reasons why you may need a custom grid. A few of the them are as follows:

- **Custom breakpoints**: It is quite common that designers decide on the responsive breakpoints in order to allow for better user experience. If that is the case, you will need to customize the breakpoints to work with the design.
- **More columns**: At times, you will need more than 12 columns, for example, 16 or even 24 columns to implement a design. With Bootstrap, you can have as many columns as you want.
- **Bigger or smaller gutters**: Sometimes, the default gutters might not work for you. In this case, you can easily adjust their size by customizing your grid.

Customizing the grid

Bootstrap uses LESS to build up its grid from the ground up, so it is fairly easy to customize it. More columns can be added to it or the size of the gutter can be changed by changing the value of a few LESS variables.

Change the number of columns in your Bootstrap project to 24 to demonstrate this by performing the following steps:

1. Open `custom-variables.less` and add the following line:

   ```
   @grid-columns: 24;
   ```

2. Recompile your styles and reload the page; you will notice your content that uses columns now only occupies half of the page. In order to compensate for it, you need to change your column definitions in `custom-theme.less` as shown in the following code snippet:

   ```
   .sidebar {
     .make-md-column(6);
     .....
   }
   .content {
     .make-md-column(18);
   }
   ```

   Once you have recompiled your styles and reloaded the page, you should see that your content looks like it did before, as shown in the following screenshot:

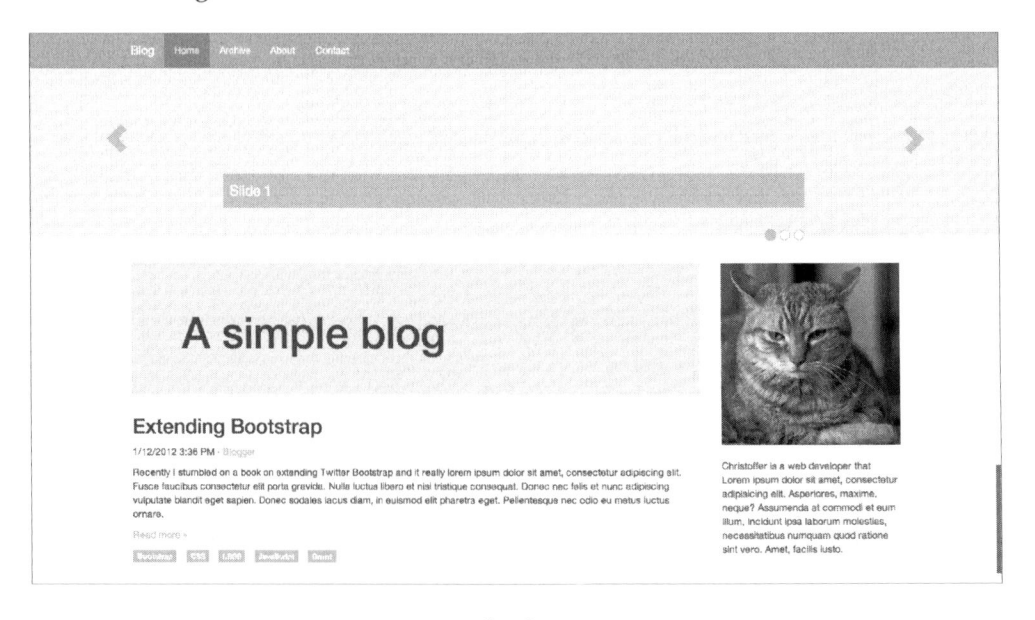

Next, take a look at how to change the size of the grid gutters by performing the following steps:

1. Open `custom-variables.less` again and add the following line of code:

   `@grid-gutter-width: 50px;`

2. Recompile your styles and reload the page to see that the space between each column is now 20 pixels larger than before, as shown in the following screenshot:

Now that you know how to do the most basic customization to the grid, it is time to look into customizing the responsive breakpoints of the grid.

Custom breakpoints

With custom breakpoints, you can control how the grid is floated on different devices. Bootstrap uses media queries to define its breakpoints, and each breakpoint can easily be customized by changing the value of its associated LESS variables.

Make some changes to the breakpoints in your Bootstrap project. Open `custom-variables.less` and add the following lines of code:

```
@screen-xs-min: 500px;
@screen-sm-min: 790px;
@screen-md-min: 1020px;
@screen-lg-min: 1240px;
```

If you now recompile your styles and reload the page, you will notice that all the breakpoints are invoked a bit later than before. This is especially useful when you have a design that requires certain breakpoints.

Next, we will take a look at how to disable responsiveness completely.

Custom Grids

Disabling responsiveness

Sometimes you may not want your site to be responsive at all, either because it targets only a single device or due to some other reason. In such cases, it is important that you know how you can disable responsiveness in Bootstrap properly.

Since the grid in Bootstrap 3 is responsive by default, you need to go through a bit more trouble than before in order to disable it. Disable responsiveness for your Bootstrap project by performing the following steps:

1. Open `index.html` and remove the following line from within the `<head>` tag:

   ```
   <meta name="viewport" content="width=device-width, initial-scale=1.0">
   ```

2. Next, remove the responsive elements from the `navbar` element:

   ```
   <nav class="navbar navbar-default" role="navigation">
     <div class="container">
       <div class="navbar-header">
         <button type="button" class="navbar-toggle" data-toggle="collapse" data-target="#bs-example-navbar-collapse-1">
           <span class="sr-only">Toggle navigation</span>
           <span class="icon-bar"></span>
           <span class="icon-bar"></span>
           <span class="icon-bar"></span>
         </button>
         <a class="navbar-brand" href="#">Blog</a>
       </div>
       <div class="collapse navbar-collapse" id="bs-example-navbar-collapse-1">
         <ul class="nav navbar-nav">
           <li class="active"><a href="#">Home</a></li>
           <li><a href="#">Archive</a></li>
           <li><a href="#">About</a></li>
           <li><a href="#">Contact</a></li>
         </ul>
       </div>
     </div>
   </nav>
   ```

3. Open `custom-theme.less` and add the following rule:

   ```
   .container {
     width: 970px !important;
   }
   ```

> Usually, you may prefer to use the extra small columns, that is, the `.col-xs-*` classes instead of the other column types. However, the other columns work as well, so you do not have to change the column types.

4. If you now recompile your styles and reload the page, you should notice that it does not stack the columns when your browser window gets smaller. This is all there is to disabling the responsiveness in Bootstrap.

Summary

In this chapter, you learned how to customize the grid in Bootstrap by changing the number of columns, resizing the grid gutters, and customizing the breakpoints. You also learned how to properly disable responsiveness in Bootstrap.

In the next chapter, you will learn about useful jQuery plugins outside Bootstrap that you can extend your project with, such as Bootbox.js, Font Awesome, and typeahead.js.

8
Custom Bootstrap Plugins

There are a lot of plugins available for Twitter Bootstrap that can be used to extend its functionality. In this chapter, we will take a closer look at some of the most popular plugins that you can use to improve the user experience in your Bootstrap projects.

Why use custom plugins?

You can save a lot of time if you use custom Bootstrap plugins instead of writing your own. Most of the popular plugins for Bootstrap receive frequent updates.

The following are some reasons why you should consider using custom plugins:

- **Saves you time**: You can always write your own plugins that go along with Bootstrap, but often someone has already done it for you, and "reinventing the wheel" is never a good thing. So look around a bit before writing any plugins yourself.
- **Stable for production**: All of the custom Bootstrap plugins mentioned in this chapter are stable for production use.
- **Frequently updated**: Most plugins are backed by some kind of community that provides ideas for improvement, helps narrow down bugs quickly, and tests new releases.

Popular plugins

As mentioned earlier, all sorts of plugins are available with Bootstrap. Some of these plugins enhance a particular Bootstrap component, while others add completely new functionality to Bootstrap.

Let us take a look at some useful plugins that you can use in your Bootstrap projects.

Bootbox.js

Bootbox (http://bootboxjs.com/) is a small jQuery plugin that uses native modals in Bootstrap, and allows you to create programmatic dialog boxes and manages them for you. It can be used to create all sorts of modals, such as normal ones, alerts, prompts, and confirms.

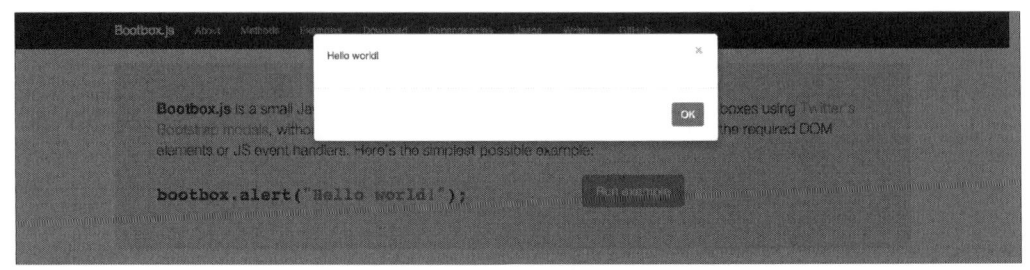

Source: http://bootboxjs.com/

Bootstrap DateTime Picker

Bootstrap DateTime Picker is a great plugin for selecting dates and date times. It has views for decades, years, months, days, hours, and minutes as well as meridian support.

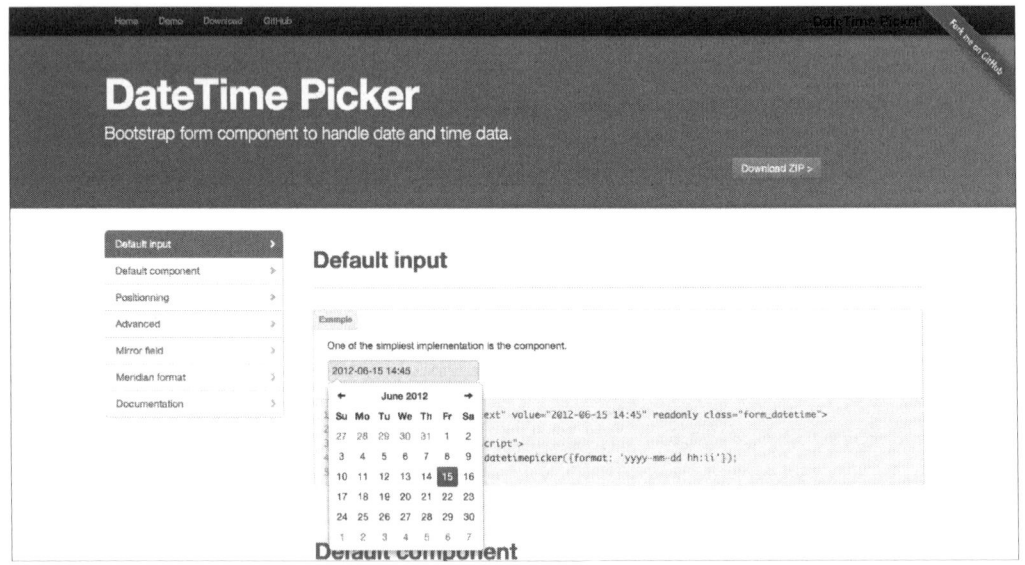

Source: http://www.malot.fr/bootstrap-datetimepicker/

Bootstrap Modal

Bootstrap Modal is an extension to the modal plugin that comes with Bootstrap. It introduces a modal manager that can handle multiple modals by listening to their events.

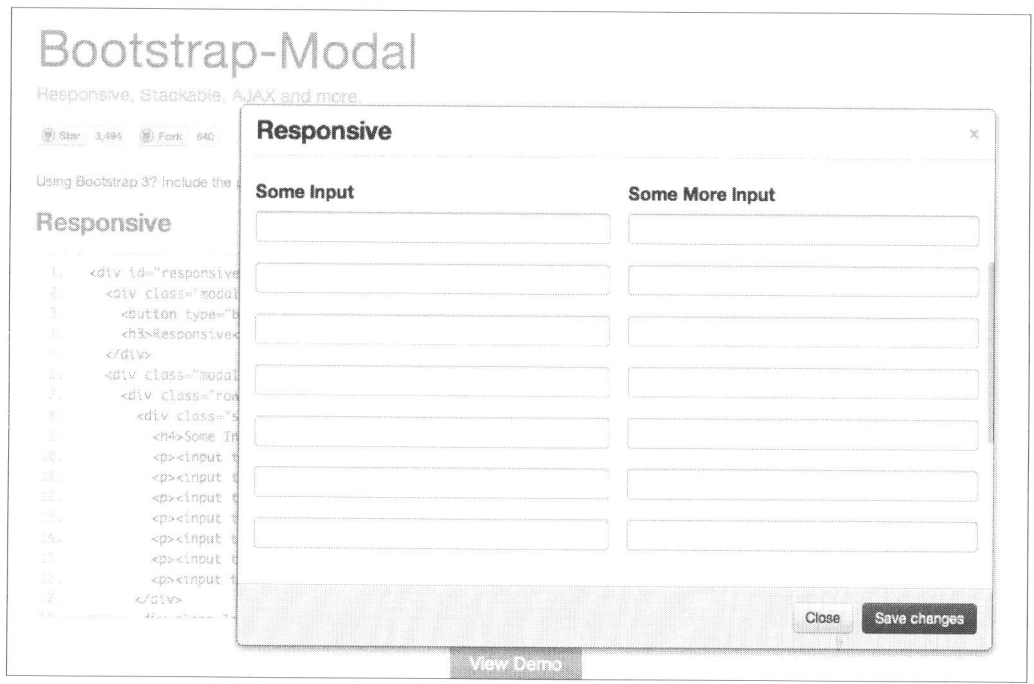

Source: http://jschr.github.io/bootstrap-modal/

Bootstrap Lightbox

Bootstrap Lightbox is a simple Lightbox plugin based on the native modal plugin in Bootstrap. It is very easy to use and supports a similar data API for native Bootstrap plugins.

Source: http://ashleydw.github.io/lightbox/

Bootstrap Wysihtml5

Bootstrap Wysihtml5 is a Bootstrap port of the popular Wysihtml5 WYSIWYG project. It provides a full-fledged WYSIWYG editor that works well with Bootstrap.

Source: https://github.com/Waxolunist/bootstrap3-wysihtml5-bower

Font Awesome

Font Awesome is an iconic font that has been designed for Bootstrap. It comes with a lot of icons that are not included in the free version of Glyphicons that comes bundled with Bootstrap.

Source: http://fortawesome.github.io/Font-Awesome/

Jasny Bootstrap

Jasny Bootstrap adds new components and JavaScript widgets to Bootstrap to provide even more building blocks. These components include the navmenu, off-canvas menu, and an excellent file input widget.

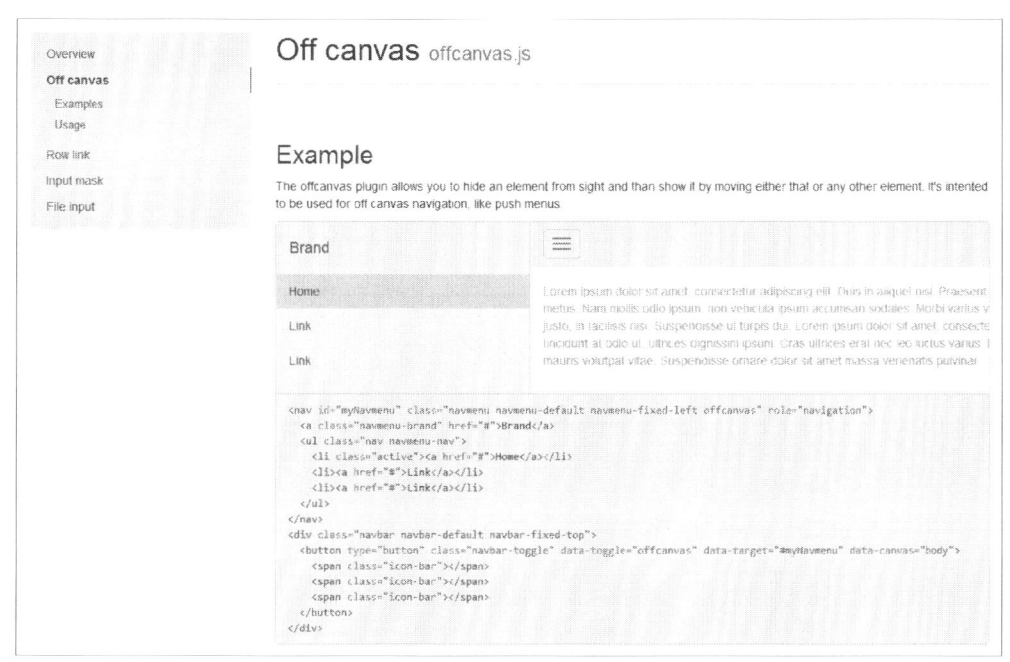

Source: http://jasny.github.io/bootstrap/

Custom Bootstrap Plugins

jQuery File Upload

jQuery File Upload is a modern file upload plugin for jQuery. It uses Bootstrap by default, but it can also be used with AngularJS and jQuery.

Source: http://blueimp.github.io/jQuery-File-Upload/

Notify.js

Notify.js is a jQuery plugin used to create notifications. It comes with a prepackaged style for Bootstrap, and you can also easily create your own style if you want to.

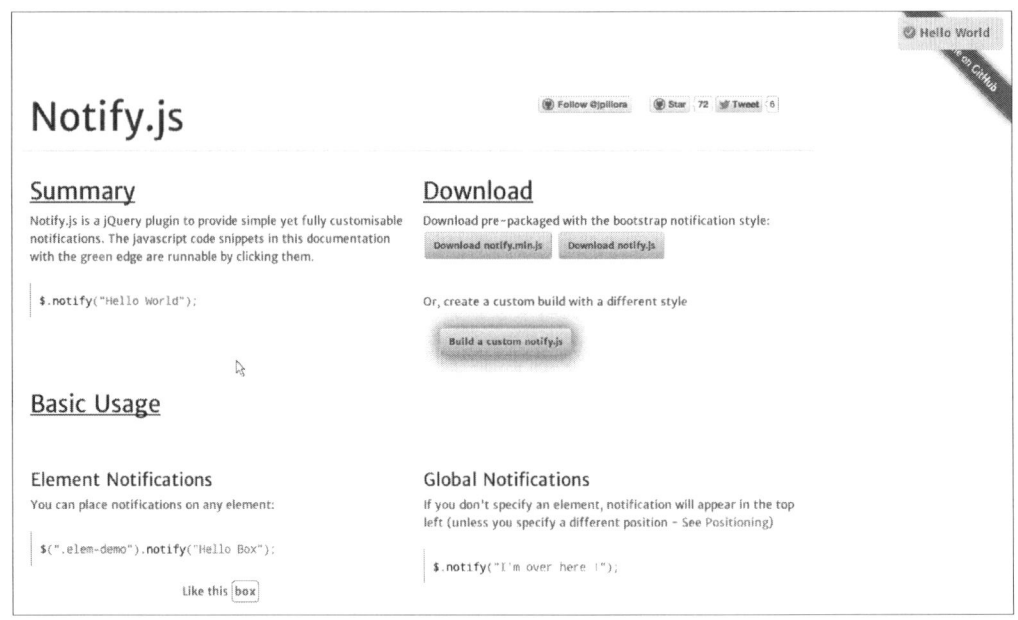

Source: http://notifyjs.com/

typeahead.js

typeahead.js is a drop-in replacement for the native autocomplete plugin in Bootstrap, which is simply not advanced enough to be used in larger projects. This full-featured autocomplete plugin was developed by Twitter engineers and can also be used without Bootstrap.

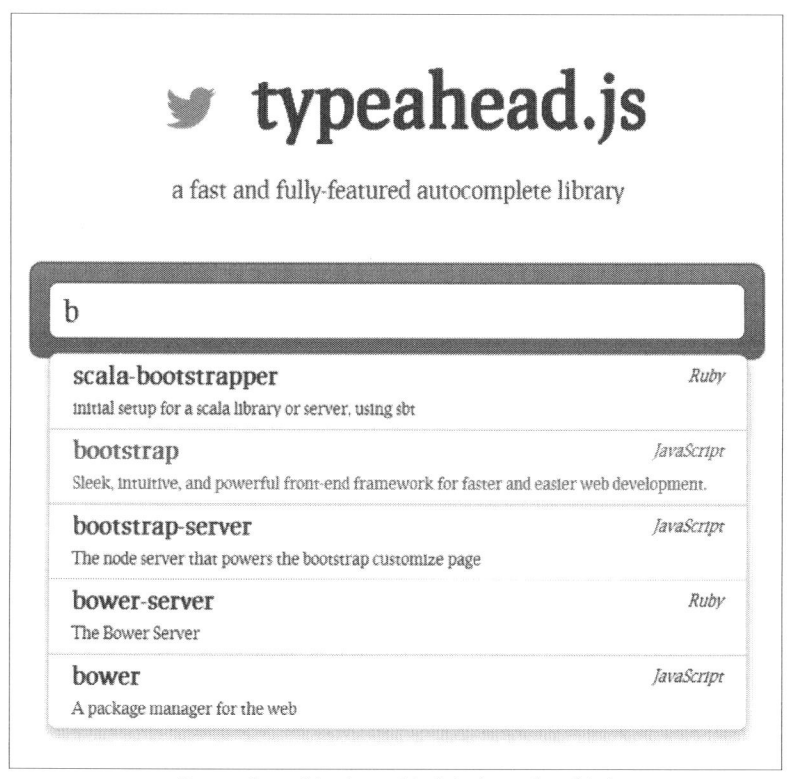

Source: http://twitter.github.io/typeahead.js/

X-editable

X-editable is the library for in-place editing on the Web. It supports all kinds of in-place editing and can be used directly with Bootstrap as well as the jQuery UI and jQuery.

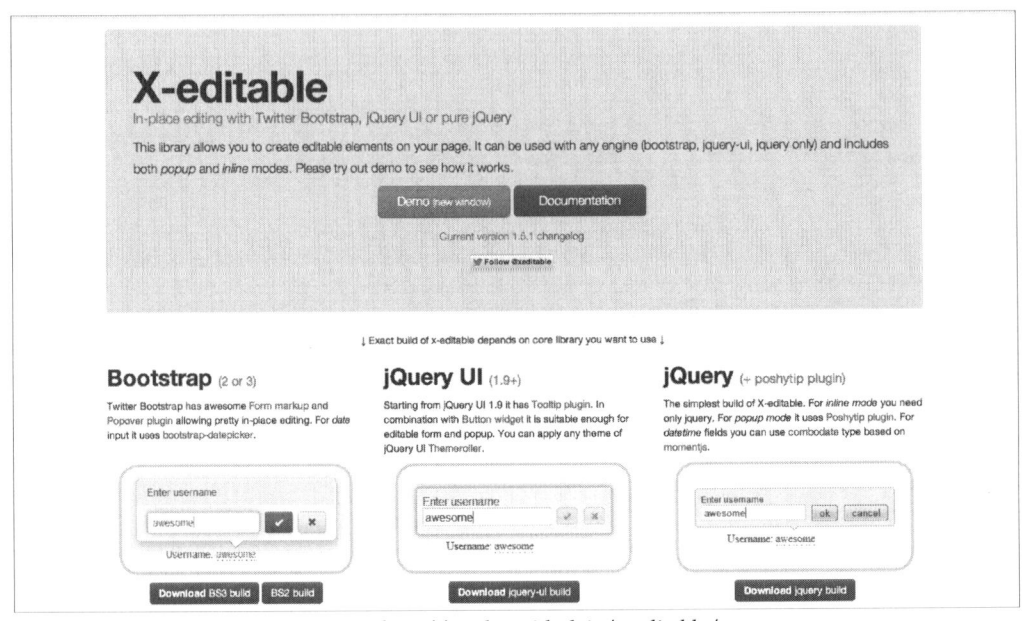

Source: http://vitalets.github.io/x-editable/

Summary

In this chapter, you learned about some useful custom plugins for Bootstrap that you can use to enhance your projects instead of creating your own plugins.

In the next chapter, you will learn how to create your own maintainable theme with the practices used in Bootswatch themes.

9
Creating Your Own Theme

Theming is an important part of customizing Bootstrap, so it is important that you learn to make your own themes in order to customize Bootstrap more efficiently. Next, you will learn why you should focus on creating original themes and how you can actually do this.

Why create a theme?

You should always try to package your customizations to Bootstrap as a standalone theme if you are working on something larger than a prototype. When you separate your theme from the rest of your styles, you can easily create more themes for the same project and re use your theme in multiple projects.

The following are some reasons why you should create your own themes:

- **Easier to maintain**: Separating your theme styles from the rest of the styles is a technique for applying a separation of concerns in your styles, and in doing so, you will find it much easier to extend and maintain your styles.
- **Standardization**: Even though Bootswatch themes are not standard, they all have the same structure and you can use this structure in all of your themes to come as close to a standard as possible.
- **Reusability**: When you separate your theme-specific styles from your other styles, you can easily copy a theme from one project to another, and better yet, you can even contribute your theme to Bootswatch.
- **Exclusivity**: Bootstrap is built with theming in mind, so there is really no reason to not separate your styles. That said, always try to create themes for your projects.

Next, we will create a theme for your Bootstrap project that separates the theme from the rest of the styles.

Creating your own Bootstrap theme

We will use Bootswatch to create our theme. You should already be familiar with Bootswatch because we used a readymade Bootswatch theme to theme our Bootstrap project earlier in this book.

Let us create a new theme. We we will name it `Greenhorn` and move the theme-specific styles and variable overrides there by performing the following steps:

1. Create a new folder under the `less` directory named `greenhorn`.
2. Create a new LESS file named `bootswatch.less` in the `greenhorn` directory and add the following contents to it:

    ```
    // Greenhorn 1.0.0
    // Bootswatch
    // -----------------------------------------------------

    // Navbar =====================================================
    // ============

    // Buttons =====================================================
    // ============

    // Typography =====================================================
    // ============

    // Tables =====================================================
    // ============

    // Forms =====================================================
    // ============

    // Navs =====================================================
    // ============

    // Indicators =====================================================
    // ============

    // Progress bars =====================================================
    // ============

    // Containers =====================================================
    // ============
    ```

> You can use this template as a starting point for your `bootswatch.less` file in all of your themes in the future.

3. Move the following styles from `custom-theme.less` to `bootswatch.less`:

   ```
   // Indicators ==========================================================

   .label {
     border-radius: 0;
   }

   .....

   // Containers ==========================================================

   .container .jumbotron {
     border-radius: 0;
   }
   ```

4. Move `custom-variables.less` to the `greenhorn` directory and rename it to `variables.less`.

   Now that you have created your theme, you can move the rest of the styles from `custom-theme.less` to `main.less` and remove `custom-theme.less` completely.

Congratulations! You have created you first Bootswatch theme! While it may not seem like much, it is a great starting point for your custom theme.

The sky's the limit! Use your imagination and create the most amazing themes. Next, you will learn how to package your theme using Bootswatch and how to share it.

Publishing your theme

Now that you have created a neat new theme for Bootstrap, you must be eager to let the world see your amazing theme. Before we can do this, you need to learn how to build your theme using Grunt. Let us set up the Bootswatch project by performing the following steps:

1. Download Bootswatch from GitHub or clone it using Git by visiting `https://github.com/thomaspark/bootswatch/`.

2. Once you have created your own copy of the Bootswatch project, you need to run the following command in the Bootswatch project root:

   `npm install`

This will install all the necessary Node.js dependencies so that you can run its Grunt tasks.

3. Copy the `greenhorn` directory into the project root and run the following command to build your theme:

   `grunt build:greenhorn`

   This will create two new files in your theme directory, `bootstrap.css` and `bootstrap.min.css`, which contain all of the Bootstrap files and customizations in your theme.

When you have built your theme, it will contain the same files as all other Bootswatch themes. If you think that your theme is good enough, you may want to consider contributing it to the Bootswatch project by doing a pull request on GitHub or selling it on WrapBootstrap (`https://wrapbootstrap.com/`).

> If you are unfamiliar with pull requests and want to learn more about them, you should read the following page from the GitHub documentation at `https://help.github.com/articles/creating-a-pull-request`.

Summary

You have now learned how to create your own theme with Bootswatch, which separates your theme styles from other styles and allows you to re use your theme in your other projects.

In this chapter, you created the `Greenhorn` theme by refactoring the styles in your Bootstrap project to follow Bootswatch conventions and learned how to share your theme.

Good job! You have finished the last chapter in this book and now have everything that you need in order to become a master at customizing Bootstrap and build awesome projects with Bootstrap.

I hope you enjoyed reading this book as much as I enjoyed writing it!

Index

B

Bootbox.js 64
Bootstrap
  about 5, 6
  advantages 23, 24
  building, from source 33, 34
  cons 7
  custom build, creating 24-26
  custom build, generating 25-27
  customizing 23, 24
  features 6
  Getting started page 9
  grid 57
  project, creating 7, 8
  pros 6
  theme 11, 71
Bootstrap DateTime Picker 64
Bootstrap JavaScript plugins. *See* **plugins**
Bootstrap Lightbox 66
bootstrap.min.css 8
Bootstrap Modal 65
Bootstrap Wysihtml5 66
Bootswatch
  used, for creating theme 72, 73

C

Cascade
  working 21
component 39
CSS3 properties 39
custom breakpoints 57-59
custom build
  creating 24

custom grid 57
custom plugins
  advantages 63

F

Font Awesome 67
functions 32

G

gradients 39
Greenhorn theme 72
grid
  about 39
  customizing 58, 59
Grunt
  benefits 41, 42
  installing 41
  LESS files, building with 41
  used, for building project 42-45
  used, for live reloading 45, 46

H

html5shiv.js 8

I

initConfig method 43

J

Jasny Bootstrap 67
jQuery File Upload 68
jQuery plugins section 25

L

LESS
  about 31, 32
  file, compiling 32, 33
less$app subtask 45
LESS components section 28
LESS files
  building, with Grunt 41, 42
LESS variables section 25, 26
live reloading
  about 42
  Grunt, using for 45

M

Mixins 31

N

nested rules 31
noConflict method 53
Node Package Manager (NPM) 32, 41
Notify.js 68
npm command 32

O

operators 32

P

plugins
  Bootbox.js 64
  Bootstrap DateTime Picker 64
  Bootstrap Lightbox 66
  Bootstrap Modal 65
  Bootstrap Wysihtml5 66
  customizing 47-50
  customizing, advantages 47, 48
  custom plugins 63
  extending 50-53
  extending, benefits 54
  Font Awesome 67
  Jasny Bootstrap 67
  jQuery File Upload 68
  Notify.js 68
  typeahead.js 69
  X-editable 70
project
  building, Grunt used 42-44

R

RECESS
  URL 33
respond.min.js 8
responsiveness
  disabling 60, 61

T

theme
  about 11, 12
  applying 14-16
  best practices 21
  creating 71
  creating, Bootswatch used 72, 73
  customizing 17-20
  publishing 73
  suitable theme, finding 13
  URL 13
typeahead.js 69

V

variables
  about 31
  customizing 34-39

W

WrapBootstrap
  URL 74

X

X-editable 70

Thank you for buying
Extending Bootstrap

About Packt Publishing

Packt, pronounced 'packed', published its first book "*Mastering phpMyAdmin for Effective MySQL Management*" in April 2004 and subsequently continued to specialize in publishing highly focused books on specific technologies and solutions.

Our books and publications share the experiences of your fellow IT professionals in adapting and customizing today's systems, applications, and frameworks. Our solution based books give you the knowledge and power to customize the software and technologies you're using to get the job done. Packt books are more specific and less general than the IT books you have seen in the past. Our unique business model allows us to bring you more focused information, giving you more of what you need to know, and less of what you don't.

Packt is a modern, yet unique publishing company, which focuses on producing quality, cutting-edge books for communities of developers, administrators, and newbies alike. For more information, please visit our website: www.packtpub.com.

About Packt Open Source

In 2010, Packt launched two new brands, Packt Open Source and Packt Enterprise, in order to continue its focus on specialization. This book is part of the Packt Open Source brand, home to books published on software built around Open Source licences, and offering information to anybody from advanced developers to budding web designers. The Open Source brand also runs Packt's Open Source Royalty Scheme, by which Packt gives a royalty to each Open Source project about whose software a book is sold.

Writing for Packt

We welcome all inquiries from people who are interested in authoring. Book proposals should be sent to author@packtpub.com. If your book idea is still at an early stage and you would like to discuss it first before writing a formal book proposal, contact us; one of our commissioning editors will get in touch with you.

We're not just looking for published authors; if you have strong technical skills but no writing experience, our experienced editors can help you develop a writing career, or simply get some additional reward for your expertise.

[PACKT] open source
community experience distilled
PUBLISHING

Twitter Bootstrap Web Development How-To

ISBN: 978-1-84951-882-6   Paperback: 68 pages

A hands-on introduction to building websites with Twitter Bootstrap's powerful front-end development framework

1. Learn something new in an Instant! A short, fast, focused guide delivering immediate results.
2. Conquer responsive website layout with Bootstrap's flexible grid system.
3. Leverage carefully-built CSS styles for typography, buttons, tables, forms, and more.

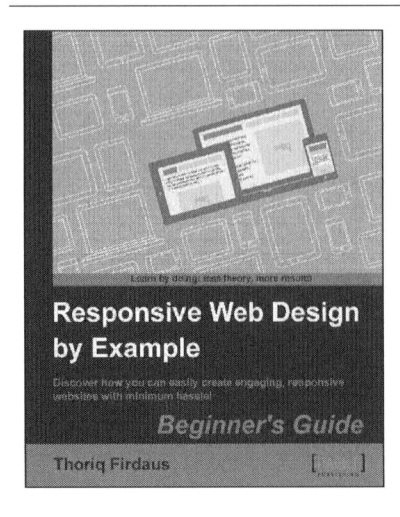

Responsive Web Design by Example Beginner's Guide

ISBN: 978-1-84969-542-8   Paperback: 338 pages

Discover how you can easily create engaging, responsive websites with minimum hassle!

1. Rapidly develop and prototype responsive websites by utilizing powerful open source frameworks.
2. Focus less on the theory and more on results, with clear step-by-step instructions, previews, and examples to help you along the way.
3. Learn how you can utilize three of the most powerful responsive frameworks available today: Bootstrap, Skeleton, and Zurb Foundation.

Please check **www.PacktPub.com** for information on our titles

Bootstrap Site Blueprints

ISBN: 978-1-78216-452-4   Paperback: 304 pages

Design mobile-first responsive websites with Bootstrap 3

1. Learn the inner workings of Bootstrap 3 and create web applications with ease.
2. Quickly customize your designs working directly with Bootstrap's LESS files.
3. Leverage Bootstrap's excellent JavaScript plugins.

Mobile First Bootstrap

ISBN: 978-1-78328-579-2   Paperback: 92 pages

Develop advanced websites optimized for mobile devices using the Mobile First feature of Bootstrap

1. Get to grips with the essentials of mobile-first development with Bootstrap.
2. Understand the entire process of building a mobile-first website with Bootstrap from scratch.
3. Packed with screenshots that help guide you through how to build an appealing website from a mobile-first perspective with the help of a real-world example.

Please check **www.PacktPub.com** for information on our titles

Printed in Great Britain
by Amazon.co.uk, Ltd.,
Marston Gate.